Oi, Pikey!

A Celebration of Cheap Living

For Mark Bainford, kind friend, generous patron, champion of the pikey cause. *

* *The authors wish to point out that they made literary history (and £70) by auctioning this dedication on eBay.*

Oi, Pikey!

A Celebration of Cheap Living

Carrie-Anne Brackstone
and Laura Bushell

HODDER &
STOUGHTON

Contents

Introduction   vii

Where Pikeys Come From   1

Pikey Timeline   3

The Etymology of Pikey   9

Heroes and Heroines   17

Anti-Pikeys   25

As You Pike It: From Cradle to Grave in Seven
Easy Steps   29

Pikey Hotspots   43

The Pikey at Play   47

The Pikey Home   49

Cheap as Chips: The Ultimate Pikey Dinner Party   55

Pastimes   63

The Pikey on TV   75

Top of the Shops   89
Can't Buy Me Love: The Lost Art of Wooing   97
The Pikey Abroad   101

The Pikey in Celebville   105
Caught in the Act: Celebrities at their Pikiest   107
Love for Sale: The Rise of the Celebrity Wedding   113
Tips from Tinseltown   119
Money for Old Rope: How to Be a Modern Artist   125
The Pikey in Vogue   131

The Future of Pikey   137
Survival of the Pikiest: Evolution and the
    Überpikey   139
Pikey Patents   143
Questionnaire   151
Pikey Manifesto   159

Glossary   162

Introduction

We Came, We Saw, We Conquered

For many years, we authors thought we were alone in our pikeyness. We felt unique in our ability to find incredibly useful items discarded in skips, inimitable in our aptitude for quoting Argos catalogue numbers off the cuff, unsurpassed in our amassed fortunes of loyalty card points. We found each other of course, one day in the supermarket reduced aisle, where we'd both beaten a path to the blue-rinsed grannies and stay-at-home mums to stage a Mexican stand-off over the last of the reduced egg sandwiches. But it was only upon further reflection (and a few probing questions to friends and family) that we realised how universal our pikey tendencies really were. Nigh on everbody is pikey whether they chose to admit it or not. We believe we've hit upon a phenomenon.

The essence of pikeyness is that it's not about how much one earns, it's about how one chooses *not* to spend it. But why has pikeyness only just come to light? How has it been kept under wraps for thousands of years? How does one become part of it? Where will it lead? Does it hurt? These are questions we felt a pressing need to investigate, because we care, and also because we thought we could make a few bob by getting a book deal.

Our in-depth research has revealed that Britain is fast becoming, nay has become, a nation of pikeys. There are more free gifts, price reductions, loyalty cards, 3-for-2s and 'buy now pay later' deals available than ever before. Pikeys watch re-runs on television, make long-distance phone calls from work, wear second-hand clothes, sue companies at the drop of a hat, steal soap from hotels and generally steer their habits towards what's cheapest. A distinct tightness of the fist has always been a trait of the British, but now we're fully embracing the pursuit of cheap thrills and grabbing at shortcuts that allow one to live life to the full without having to shell out for it.

This book, therefore, is our call to arms. Within these pages we present you with our exploration into the world of the pikey. We hope you will both recognise yourself and discover invaluable tips to improve your pikey performance. We will bring you face to face with some of the proud traditions of pikeyness, its influence, the pikey followers and the exciting possibilities of the future. It's time for you, dear readers, to wear your pikeyness on your polyester sleeve, hold your Cash 'n' Carry card aloft and declare 'I am Pikey and Proud!'

Where Pikeys Come From

Pikey Timeline

In order to begin to understand the pikey, it is necessary to revisit the annals of history with a completely open mind. This revisionist attitude may seem a little extreme, but given the way that pikey history has been sidelined by the educational system, we feel it our duty to inform the masses. The more observant reader will notice that the seventies was a boon, a veritable renaissance, for the pikey. It is also the decade in which we were both born. Mere coincidence or divine providence? You decide.

.99p

0027
Jesus turns water in to wine.

1538
Elizabeth I grants special privileges for the collection of rags for papermaking, which in turn creates the Rag and Bone Man.

1841
German brothers Clemens and August form C&A, now a leading European fashion retailer whose name is synonymous with cheap chic.

1890
In Preston, the first H Samuel opens its doors. Today, with over 430 stores it is firmly established as the UK's favourite high street jeweller and retailer of cheap bling.

1917
Rationing is introduced during the First World War. Many resent cutting back on food, but die-hard pikeys make a mint by selling their excess grub on the black market.

1530
The Italian National Lottery, the inspiration for modern bingo, is organised. Today it remains indispensable to the Italian government's budget with a yearly contribution in excess of 75 million dollars. Only pikeys twig that this is a rip-off.

1885
In Paris the first flea market came into being. The French are so classy they call their rag and bone men 'pêcheurs de lune' (moon fishermen), while in England we call them 'bin-divers'.

1911
Parliament introduce the dole. Pikeys hand in their notice and try to live off the state for as long as possible.

1930
Jan Kip invents the caravan. Not quite cars and not quite vans but houses on wheels.

1947
Oxfam, the first charity shop opens. There are now over 6500 charity shops in the UK alone where even rich people shop, re-branding their charity buys as vintage couture.

1947
The first commercial microwave hits the market. This is why frozen rice and sausages that cook in 1 minute exist.

1958
The BBC broadcast Blue Peter. A programme dedicated to making just about anything from old tat and coining the phrase, 'Here's one I made earlier.'

1970
The first Iceland freezer shop opens in Oswestry. There are now over 760 stores in the UK with plans to open 80 more stores in the next 3 years. If it moves, freeze it.

1973
Argos opens its first store. There are now over 540 stores throughout the UK and Republic of Ireland. Approximately 98% of the UK population live within 10 miles of an Argos store. How reassuring.

1974
Package holidays become affordable for the ordinary family, so pikeys run amok around the world.

1975
Chas and Dave release their first album 'One Fing 'n' Annuver. The rest is history . . .

1977
The Antiques Roadshow is first broadcast in the UK spawning hundreds of mercenary bargain hunters and an equal amount of forged antiques.

1977
The UK's staple diet, Pot Noodle, hits the supermarket shelves.

1977
The ultimate gourmet snack, cheese, onion and pineapple on sticks, begins to make an appearance at only the most exclusive of cocktail parties.

1981
Poundstretcher opens in the UK, offering quality women, men and children's clothing for just over ninety-nine pence.

1986
QVC Inc. was founded in 1986 by Joseph Segel, A virtual shopping mall that never closes – QVC is a place where customers can, and do, shop at any hour – at the rate of two customers per second. Themed programs are telecast live 24 hours a day, seven days a week, to 84 million house-holds in the United States. Gold plated jewellery and portable curtain steamers suddenly seem like a good idea.

1988
Car boot sale mania sweeps the UK. People revel in the idea of getting money for things they would otherwise have burned, others like the idea of buying cheap things and then burning them.

1990
Student loans introduced in the UK, inducing much piss-artistry amongst young intellectuals who have access to vodka at 50p a shot.

1994
The National Lottery is first played in the UK.The Government have clearly been talking to the Italians (see 1530).

1995
eBay is founded in Pierre Omidyar's San Jose living room. The birth of the virtual car boot sale and the start of many a career as a modern day spiv.

1995

The first booking taken by easyJet on 23 October, as the easyJet telephone reservation centre opens at easyLand, the home of easyJet at London Luton Airport. easyPeasy.

2001

36 people attempt to sue McDonald's after the famous coffee spilling lawsuit in the US. High Court Justice Richard Field said McDonald's has no obligation to warn customers about the risk of scalding from a beverage that's made from boiling water. Hard luck pikeys.

2005

A bargain-induced frenzy hits the opening of Britain's largest IKEA when 6,000 customers decide it's a good idea to descend upon Edmonton in the hope of bagging a £45 sofa. Scuffles break out amongst the covetous flat-pack furniture fans and police clear the shop after just half an hour, no doubt stopping to pick up a nice lamp for the missus on the way out.

1995

TESCO is the first supermarket to introduce the loyalty card. Others will follow, we have a feeling.

1996

BBC broadcasts the first home makeover show, 'Changing Rooms'. MDF becomes a household name, contestants end up with bright orange living rooms, builders lose work.

2004

A couple are the first to marry in ASDA after meeting in the supermarket. They have the ASDA theme tune played by a lone piper as they tie the knot.

2005

Glastonbudget, the no frills music festival is launched. Boldly going where real bands wouldn't be seen dead, tribute bands throw themselves to the mercy of ale-drinking pikeys.

The Etymology
of Pikey

CHEAP!

Pikey is not a term to be taken lightly. It is a compliment of the highest degree and while we're sure that it will soon be the word on the lips of the glitterati, the literati and just about everyone else, we're also aware of its very shady roots. Pikey has for many years stood as an insult towards people of no fixed abode who've taken flak for not investing in bricks and mortar. Thus we are also fully aware that the mere title of our tome will have sent many a bookshop-browser off in a fit of apoplexy.

But it is not our wish to perpetuate the ignorance of the bigoted and misinformed; to hell with them: language is changing with the times and in recent years pikey has moved on to higher echelons of usage. Like a phoenix rising from the ashes, pikey has cast off its politically incorrect roots and come to mean something quite contrary to its original usage. If you're still unsure, think how the meaning of expressions such as 'wicked', 'sound' or 'mint' have changed. Pikey has been around since the 15th-century, here's how it got to where it is today.

✳ Turnpike

A spiked barrier fixed in or across a road or passage, as a defence against sudden attack, esp. of men on horseback.

This cropped up in around 1420 in *Siege of Rouen*:

 'He made a dyche of grete coste, Pyght with stakys that wolde perysce, With turnepykys, and with many an hers.'

Well, it makes no sense to us either, but for the sake of historical accuracy it is apparently the earliest record of the word. Turnpikes were a kind of gate, often a horizontal piece of wood on a vertical pin, that kept horses off the footpaths or cattle out of streams and waterways, much like a modern turnstile. That's all very well, but the turnpike really becomes of interest to us when it is used to make a few bob:

A barrier, later a gate or gates, placed across a road to stop passage till the toll is paid; a toll-gate, a turnstile.

This appeared in 1695 when turnpikes were a regular feature of the nation's roads. Turnpikes were guarded by turnpike-keepers who extorted a small fee from travellers wishing to pass through the gate. (It's now that the first whiffs of pikeyness begin to emerge.) Charles Dickens was a great fan of the turnpike and he made a point of featuring it in many of his novels, such as 1863's *The Unconventional Traveller*:

 'The Turnpike-house was all overgrown with ivy; and the Turnpike-keeper, unable to get a living out of the tolls, plied the trade of a cobbler.'

Notice how the cobbler has two jobs on the go at once – fixing shoes in between working the turnpike to optimise his labour/profits ratio no doubt. Very pikey.

Turnpiker

One who frequents the turnpike or turnpike road; a foot-traveller; turnpike sailor.

This is more like it. The first reference to turnpikers appeared in 1791 and they were travellers who traipsed along highways and byways and got caught for a fee every time they passed a turnpike. This presumably left them pretty skint after a few days on the road, hence in August 1812 the *Boston Gazette* referred to 'turnpikers, unaccoutred and undisciplined'.

Pike

1) Short for Turnpike: A bar or gate on a road at which toll is collected; a toll-bar or toll-gate.

This shortened version was presumably in oral use for a great many years before it was recorded by the turnpike's greatest fan; yep, it's Dickens again, this time in *The Pickwick Papers*:

'I dewote the remainder of my days to a pike.'

This declaration of adoration for the pike came in 1837 and Dickens used the word later in the same novel to mean the toll paid at the turnpike. But he just couldn't let it stand and was only satisfied when he dropped in yet another mention of the word:

'"What do you mean by a pike-keeper?" inquired Mr Peter Magnus. "The old 'un means a turnpike keeper, gen'lm'n," observed Mr Weller, in explanation.'

2) To make off with oneself, go away quickly, be off. To depart; to proceed or go. Also to pike it.

Malory used pike in this sense in his tales of Arthurian romance, *Le Morte D'Arthur* (1470–85):

'And thenne anone that damoysel pyked her away pryuely.'

Sounds very romantic indeed; what a lady. But 'piking away' later evolved into the delightful phrase 'pike off!' which we believe should be brought back into contemporary usage. This came about in 1825 and has essentially the same meaning as 'bugger off', 'sod off', 'piss off' and every other phrase ending in 'off' which means 'go away'.

In 1889 the word 'pike' began to take on some of the significance that 'pikey' has today:

3) To shirk; to hold back; to back out.

In John S. Farmer's 1889 tome *Americanisms*, this was attributed to one who is backwards in coming forwards when it comes to gambling:

> *'To pike – to play cautiously and for small amounts, never advancing the value of the stake . . . Those who gamble in this fashion are called pikers.'*

This is extremely close to the contemporary pikey school of thought in that it involves parting with as little cash as possible. But as it also involves small returns and still a small amount of risk it is also rare amongst die-hard pikeys.

4) Term of contempt on the Pacific Coast for a person of no means or of migratory habits; a poor white; a thief.

Pike County in Missouri was where the first of these unfortunates were said to have originated before they relocated to California. The first written record of this abusive term was in 1854 but novelist Charles Nordhoff summed up its sentiments perfectly in 1872:

> *'The true Pike, however, in the Californian sense of the word, is the wandering, gipsy-like southern poor white.'*

And in 1946 the *St Louis Globe-Democrat* reported:

> *'The term 'Pike' or 'piker', in the sense of a worthless, lazy, good-for-nothing person arose first in California.'*

One gets the feeling they weren't welcomed with open arms.

✳ Piker

A vagrant, a tramp; a gypsy.

In 1838 William Holloway's *Dictionary of Provincialisms* described the piker as follows:

'Cadgers and pikers are tramps.'

Blunt but to the point. 'Piker' is also in use in the United States, Australia and New Zealand today where it has come to mean a lazy person, a shirker, or someone who is downright fecking useless.

Pikey

So here we are, already so soon. Or not. 'Pikey' has been in use as long as turnpikes have existed and so we as authors are incredibly grateful to those little gates otherwise we wouldn't be making a pikey fortune by writing a book about pikeyness. Ahem. Let's look at its usage, namely in J. O. Halliwell's *Dictionary of Archaic and Provincial Words* (1847):

'Piky, a gipsey. Kent.'

That's it: the conception. In 1887's *Dictionary of Kentish Dialect*, an indispensable volume if ever there was such a thing, 'pikey' features as follows:

'Piky, a turnpike traveller; a vagabond; and so generally a low fellow.'

And latterly in 1955 in Peter Wildeblood's *Against the Law*:

'My family's all Pikeys, but we ain't on the road no more!'

'Pikey' still clings onto its archaic meaning even today. As a term of abuse for travelling folk it has quite rightly been deemed politically incorrect. BBCi News reported that it had been banned from use by the police as it stood to describe:

'a particular type of criminal usually from the travelling community'.

Shame they didn't ban 'you're', 'under' and 'arrest' as that would have saved many law-breaking pikeys the misfortune of having to spend time inside. Though thinking of the money saved on bills, doing a stretch could be a blessing in disguise.

But pikey has evolved beyond this into a term for the way in which our society is desperate to save money. It is not limited to a certain class but is present across the board, identifiable by certain traits that denote a frugal attitude towards cashflow issues. Tim Lott in the *Evening Standard* described the new meaning of 'pikey' as follows:

'A pikey, usually a disparaging term for a traveller, has come to mean something quite different in my household. Pikeyness is a state of mind. It's a kind of cheeseparing, bargain-hunting disposition that often goes beyond the bounds of reason. Pikeys collect air miles, hoard coupons and have more loyalty cards than you'll find in a pack of playing cards. Pikeys buy things they don't need because they're on three-for-two offer. They buy clothes in sales not because they like them, but because they are half-price . . .'

Over 150 years since its inception, pikey continues to shock and awe. We can only hope to add to its legacy with one final definition:

pikey *('paiki) n. one averse to spending money who finds cheap, creative or morally reprehensible alternatives, hatches plans, or just goes without.*

Heroes and Heroines

Now that we've established the pikey's place in the evolution of the human race, it's time to turn towards those well-known historical figures who have displayed a penchant for pikeyness that was truly ahead of their time. These forward-thinkers were often unaware that their actions fell within the parameters of pikey or that they were making such a massive contribution to this aspect of society. But the fact that so many influential people adopt either the whole pikey lifestyle package or tenets of its teaching serves to illustrate its importance. Working in various disciplines, these heroes and heroines radiate pikeyness to an awe-inspiring extent. We salute them!

.99p

✳ Jesus Christ

A humble upbringing, persecution, and the ability to throw together a feast on a budget made Jesus the ultimate pious pikey. Wooing the crowds with his water-into-wine party trick, his status as pikey miracle-maker was affirmed further still when he turned bread and fish into tuna sandwiches for the masses. Many a feckless pikey has tried to emulate his catering skills but to no avail; it seems he was in a league of his own.

✳ Robin Hood

Nottingham's most famous export, Robin Hood is the pikey saviour *par excellence*. Together with his band of Merry Men, Robin was not only a very successful robber but he donated the proceeds from his avid pillaging of the rich to those living less salubriously. Defending the underdog against oppression, he was the first ambassador for pikey rights. What a nice young man.

✳ Thérèse Humbert

Humble country girl Thérèse Humbert took 19th-century French society for a ride when she pretended to be the illegitimate child of a billionaire and heiress to a fortune. Society fell over themselves to lend her money and treat her like a queen, assuming they would one day be paid back. Little did they know the cheeky minx was lying and in reality didn't have two pennies, or should that be centimes, to rub together. *Le pikey – c'est magnifique!*

✳ Charlie Chaplin

A cinematic icon, Chaplin made a career out of dressing as a vagabond. The ultimate low-maintenance chap, the Little Tramp was created when Chaplin stole the entire outfit from other people's wardrobes – Fatty Arbuckle for one lost a pair of trousers. He then went on to make a mint, but even as a millionaire Chaplin continued to live in a shabby hotel room and stowed all of his sizeable cheques away in a suitcase. Whether or not he replaced Arbuckle's missing trousers remains a mystery.

✳ The Old Woman Who Lived in a Shoe

A shoe – what a masterstroke of cheap housing from this stingy mum. She had so many children she didn't know what to do (stop sleeping around, perhaps?), so she fed them all on broth, scrimped on bread, and sent them off to bed with no TV, squandering their considerable child allowance on lottery tickets, hoping that one day she'd be able to retire to a nice big knee-high boot in the country.

✳ HRH Queen Elizabeth II

Royalty is a highly aspirational position for the pikey, and being the Queen is the pinnacle of low-expenditure living. Freebies include a palace, a variety of country retreats, servants, a choice of the most expensive clothes, foods, jewellery and cars. Need we go on? All for being born in the right place at the right time. Even her pooches enjoy a level of pampering that the pikey can only dream of. Watch and learn.

✳ Chas 'n' Dave

Everyone's favourite cockney geezers, the boys have exceeded in promoting frugal East End values through their very own brand of rock 'n' roll with songs such as 'Gambler', 'Scruffy Old Cow', 'Ponders End Allotments Club' and 'Margate' under their beer-belly-strained belts. Their records occupying a cherished place in every mockney's sideboard, Chas 'n' Dave's rough 'n' ready attitude has earned a well-deserved place in our hearts. And they'd have Blue in a fight any day. Woortcha!

✳ Ken Dodd

A much-loved British comedian, Dodd made the humble feather duster his comedy trademark. He also utilised his distinct lack of dentistry and unruly hair to his advantage by incorporating them into his cheaply maintainable comic image. Another follower of a spartan lifestyle, Dodd's humble up-bringing infiltrated his entire life despite his amassed riches. In the eighties Dodd famously went on trial for tax evasion but was acquitted, claiming he was just bad at maths.

⁎ Catherine Zeta-Jones

Our very own Catherine the Great is a prime example of how no amount of fame or fortune can change a tight-fisted Welshie. From her humble origins in Swansea, Catherine Z-J has become an advocate of the joys of cheap living amongst the Hollywood elite, even going so far as to infiltrate the Douglas family to convert them into penny-pinchers. And it seems to be working – note the well-documented shopping trips to MFI and Argos. Mission accomplished.

⁎ Jordan

Despite her erotically charged image, page 3 stunner Jordan is an example of brains behind beauty. Jordan illustrates the type of savviness that sees one investment reap multitudinous rewards. By ploughing a few thousand pounds into various breast enlargement operations, Jordan counted on the fact that she could rake in a fortune by having extraordinarily large jugs. And hasn't she just? Raked in a fortune, that is.

⁎ Jerry Springer

Jerry Springer is the king of the tacky talk show who invented the concept of turning other people's problems into prime-time TV and making a great deal of money off the back of it. People who are pregnant by their boyfriend's transsexual mum fight it out with their brother's boyfriend's Nazi lovechild in front of the nation, who cheer even more if they throw chairs at each other. Jerry spuriously suggests at the end of each show that viewers should take care of themselves and, of course, each other.

☀ David Blaine

Millionaire magician David Blaine took pikeyness to the extreme when he locked himself into a glass box suspended over the Thames for 44 days. Mind over matter meant Blaine did not eat for the duration of the stunt, saving a fortune on food bills, as well as receiving some kind donations of eggs and tomatoes from passers-by. He also stood to make a fortune from media coverage once he emerged from his box. Genius.

☀ Stelios

The pikey's favourite when it comes to travelling across Europe without breaking into a fiver, Stelios stopped just short of having passengers travel on wind-up aeroplanes to bring us cheap travel. He's now trying to conquer the world to bring us everything we need in his trademark no-frills, low-budget, orange-branded form – cars, food, even men's toiletries. We're looking forward to easyMoney and easyLay. Gotta dream, folks.

☀ Ingvar Kamprad

The man who taught us the Scandinavian for value, Kamprad founded his IKEA empire aged seventeen using a cheque his dad gave him for being good at school. He's now one of the richest men on earth, but likes to save money by travelling second-class, living tax-free in Switzerland and shopping for bargains at his local market. He's so clever, he can even assemble a BILLY bookcase in less than three hours, without the instructions, and get the shelves the right way round.

Anti-Pikeys

Tis the way of the world that for every Danger Mouse there must be a Baron Silas Greenback. And so it follows that for each pikey hero and heroine there is an anti-pikey, the antagonist whose every move is dictated by the need to undermine pikey ideals, who spits bile at the existence of pikeyness as we know it. Where this venom comes from is a mystery, but these folks just don't go in for the whole pikey thing.

.99p

The Ancient Greeks

'Oooh look! A big wooden horse!
You shouldn't have!' Yes, we're
talking about the nasty trick that
the Greeks played on the Trojans
when they left an oversized horse-
on-wheels outside the gates of
Troy. They knew that no pikey
could resist such an extravagant
freebie and that the Trojans would
be just itching to steal it. Then
they sneaked out from inside their
so-called 'gift' and slaughtered the
Trojans in their sleep. Charming.

Margaret Thatcher

Not only did the Iron Lady advocate the use of hairspray on
a devastating scale, but the policies she inflicted on Great
Britain during her reign almost sent the pikey populous pack-
ing. The Welfare State was the linchpin of pikey living and
Thatcher made massive cutbacks to its infrastructure, paving
the way for capitalism. The result of this was that many a
pikey benefit-lover had to actually go out and find a job. Eeevil.

Bill Gates

One of the richest men in the world, Bill Gates has made an
absolute fortune by convincing almost the whole of Western

civilisation (and then some) that we need to use computers for everything. What's wrong with the good old paper and pen? Who knows. But still we have to keep upgrading, downloading, and debugging as Bill and his smug animated paperclip dictate. He is the puppet master from whom all pikeys must be liberated. Stick that in your spreadsheet and smoke it!

✳ The Milkybar Kid

Apparently, only the best is good enough for this fussy little upstart. In he rides, so clean cut that he looks like he's been through a hot wash, trying to make friends with all the other poncy kids by handing over a truckload of white chocolate bars and making like he's the most generous person in the world. Pretentious little shit!

✳ P. Diddy

Bling, in its purest designer form, is the antithesis of pikeyness. Puff Daddy aka Puffy aka Sean Coombs aka P. Diddy not only wastes valuable time and effort on having too many names but his conspicuous consumption represents a flagrant disregard for the benefits of being pikey. If he just went down Walthamstow market for all that gold and bought Cava instead of Cristal he'd save a fortune. But no; he must spend, spend, spend like there's no tomorrow.

As You Pike It:
CHEAP! Cradle to Grave in Seven Easy Steps

All the world's a giant cut-price supermarket, and all the men and women merely pikeys. Each has their vouchers and forged banknotes, their loyalty points and credit vouchers, and in his time one pikey commits many scams. The life cycle of a pikey is a curious thing, in some ways so similar to that your average Brit, but in other ways so much more interesting. With both nature and nurture playing their part, it's fascinating to see how the pikey evolves to suit each of the seven stages of its life, each time adopting the new pikey skills needed to negotiate the ups and downs that a stint on God's own Earth throws before us. Frankly, we're amazed.

.99p

Given their parentage, it's clear from the outset that the pikelet has the potential to become something big in the world of pikeydom. Infancy is a key stage for indulging and honing the pikelet's skills as the screaming, gibbering, demanding sprog makes the most of having parents on tap to cater for its every need. However, it's equally important that the pikey parent exploits this impressionable stage in the pikelet's formative years.

Dressed in hand-me-downs and jumble-sale chic, the pikelet soon learns to disregard fashion and ignore the sniggering that accompanies their every appearance in public. Transgender outfits from various decades in itchy fabrics are de rigueur and the pikelet will grow up believing that a combination of pink velvet trousers, a Free Nelson Mandela t-shirt and fluorescent jelly shoes is cool.

The pikelet will be taken under duress to places where under-5s go free and forced to enjoy things they blatantly have no interest in. If anyone asks, they are under strict instructions to be $4\frac{1}{2}$, even when they're 10. Other kids' birthday parties are a chance to off-load the pikelets and teach them a valuable lesson in exploiting the generosity of others. Coma-inducing quantities of coke floats, rice krispie cakes, and Arctic roll must be consumed before making off with eight party bags and the coveted pass-the-parcel prize.

Pikelets will eat anything, including worms, mud and cat food. However, to avoid the wrath of Social Services, they should be weaned onto legitimately foul economy food such as fish fingers, iced fingers, chocolate fingers, sponge fingers, sugar sandwiches and cherryade until the E-numbers give them brain damage. The more health-conscious amongst pikey parents may choose the lentil and beansprout approach, which enables their children to waste away through pure culinary boredom.

It should also be instilled in the impressionable pikelet that the imagination is the most powerful form of entertainment. Low expectations and a love of cheap thrills can be cultivated through denial of expensive toys, replaced instead with egg boxes, string and dried-up felt-tip pens. Additional tricks, such as pretending the ice cream van only plays music when it's empty, ensure the minimum of outgoings when raising a pikelet.

✳ Step 2: The Pikey Goes to School (or Not)

Striking out on their own for the first time, starting school is when the pikelet learns to make friends and influence people, especially their minted classmates. The pikelet is fully aware that school is the perfect testing ground for the skills that they will later come to rely on and that at this tender age they are, most crucially, out of reach of the long arm of the law.

While other kids busy themselves with *The Hungry Caterpillar,* this young pikey concentrates on the more valuable life skills of racketeering, entrepreneurialism and extortion. The only reason they turn up to school is to exploit the weaknesses of their naïve and needy contemporaries, who'll readily swap their brand new Nike trainers for a stolen air gun and a Dairylea Triangle.

Bunking off affords the young pikey the opportunity to shoplift, develop a taste for cheap fags, and drink white cider until they puke. Such experiences are invaluable and something you would never get at school. Thus the young pikey is worldly beyond his years, and has probably been to rehab before most children have a clue what it means.

The young pikey is happiest in his natural habitat: the park or bus shelter, where grunting can pass as conversation and young pikeys en masse can talk about going to the market and buying fake designerwear. On a good day there'll even be a porn magazine abandoned in the undergrowth, which the young pikey can then take home, dry out on the radiator, and loan out to his horny young friends for £2 an hour.

An enthusiastic collector for various sham charities, the young pikey avidly fund-raises for such worthy causes as the Spectacles for Fish Foundation and the R. Sole Institute for Tourette's Sufferers. Friends and neighbours have learnt to donate generous amounts of cash and regularly endure bouts of out-of-season carol singing and overly aggressive trick-or-treating, lest things get 'nasty'.

☀ Step 3: The Pikey at University – the Golden Years

For most students, university is the first rung on the ladder towards adulthood and success, a chance to grow up and get qualified. For the pikey student, the lure of tax-free living and the number of freebies available is more enticing than a night down Walthamstow Dogs with Jodie Marsh. Armed with a Student Loan application, a second-hand copy of *Grub on a Grant* and their dead granny's Breville sandwich maker, the student pikey is ready to optimise their pikey virility at this crucial stage of their freeloading life.

Beware of standing downwind of this species, as the odour of the great unwashed can be quite overwhelming. Pikey students will only use the laundrette as a last resort, i.e. when they have worn all their pants forwards, backwards and inside-out. The more frivolous amongst them will splash out on a bottle of Febreze.

Stealing toilet roll from pubs, scrabbling for change down the side of the sofa, using coupons from magazines, and stealing food and clothing from friends are all popular pastimes whilst at university. Pikey points can be accrued by stretching out the credit on one electricity key to accommodate a reasonable amount of cooking, light and television-watching time without paying over the odds. When times are hard and there's not a single IKEA nightlight in the house for warmth and light, one-night-stands, even with the college trog, are a viable option.

Clearly, all sense of taste and decency has been extinguished in the pikey at this stage. Three-for-twos and BOGOFs are the epicentre of any shopping experience and at the supermarket cheap and very unhealthy food is always on the menu. Pot Noodles, Super Noodles, turkey burgers, value baked beans, and mechanically recovered meat products made from knobbly bits of cow, pig and Alsatian are popular options. All have been 'Brevilled' at one time or another.

Alcohol consumption on a par with Oliver Reed is a nightly activity achieved on a tight budget by imbibing nauseous cocktails, alcopops (that are strangely not so popular in commercial bars), snakebite & black, and vodka jelly.

Daytime is spent recovering in a sleeping bag in front of *Trisha* and *This Morning*.

✻ Step 4: The Pikey Gets Laid

When it comes to wooing, the amorous pikey is the first to remind their date that money can't buy you love. When their thoughts turn to romance, both the Pike and Pikette have one thing in mind: the cheap date and easily pleased mate. Although at first glance Pike and Pikette may seem made for each other, their shared interest in freeloading off their respective partner proves fatal to their relationship and inevitably leads to fisticuffs.

The Pike – The term 'low-maintenance' was invented for the Pike, who has been wearing the same Guns 'n' Roses t-shirt since his teens and thinks body odour is 'manly'. His unshaven, shaggy-haired charm is a hit with the ladies, who often find themselves out of pocket after paying for a night on the beers with him. Pike has opted out of the rat race and earns a living as an artist/musician/writer or any arty occupation that might sound 'deep' and 'a struggle' and affords him much sympathy from girls. In reality he is on the dole and his only artistic bent is towards forgery. Pike likes a petite lady, so that on her birthday he can buy her a nice children's outfit and not have to pay tax on it. Petite ladies, with an appetite to match: Pike thinks there's nothing worse than a woman who eats lots and can hold her drink, it's just so unladylike (and expensive).

The Pikette – A purveyor of what has been politely labelled 'boho chic', a look that gained kudos when sported by various celebrities, Pikette's look is directional, as is her attitude. Throwing scorn in the face of Women's Lib, she yearns for a relationship where the man pays the bills, buys the house, gives her an allowance, and she gets to stay at home and breed. In Pikette's world a man is a protector, and it always amazes her how many chumps fall for her 'damsel in distress' routine. Though happiest when fleecing unsuspecting men for all they can give, she can't resist a brawl when things get competitive at her local boot sale or in the reduced section of Waitrose – boyf's paying so she goes posh.

✳ Step 5: The Pikey Gets Paid

While many a dole bludger may be harbouring the illusion that they're living the idler's dream, any pikey worth their salt knows that having a job, getting paid to slack off and run an internet business on the side with the added bonus of paid holidays, sick leave, and an expenses account is the way forward. With some careful planning, it is possible to forge the perfect pikey career.

Rag-and-Bone Man

While cries of 'Any old iron!' ringing out from some old bugger driving a knackered old van down your street may be a thing of the past, the rag-and-bone man (or woman, for that matter) is still very much in existence. In their modern incarnations, RBMs spend their weekends hawking around car boot sales and will utilise the information superhighway to flog their pikey wares on eBay. They swoop like vultures on house clearance sales and reclamation centres. If it's not nailed down they'll have it.

Spiv

The modern spiv takes on many forms, from the used-car salesman to ticket tout or the man on the street selling 'genuine' designer watches from a suitcase (NB the hands drop off and they stain your wrist green within no time). Whatever knocked-off goods they're trying to flog, however, these pikeys all have one thing in common: the uncanny knack of disappearing in the presence of the law. Now, if they had only said they were selling invisibility capes we would have definitely had one.

Corporate Minion

Many may scoff at the oppression, exploitation and general lack of fun that goes with joining a top-dollar, multi-national corporation, but the true pikey doesn't wince when it comes to surrendering his soul to capitalism. Searching out the company that offers the most freebies, this pikey will whole-heartedly lay every facet of his meagre life at the sacrificial altar. The price may be high, but think of all those gifts – gym membership, eye tests, holidays, health insurance, theatre tickets, therapy for the inevitable nervous breakdown – and just try to resist.

Media Whore

Finely tuned instruments of pikeyness, those pikeys working in the media are poised to pounce on anything that might be free, especially if it involves getting drunk or high. They'll work through a launch party, wrap party, premiere party, Z-list celebrity's birthday party, stripping it of booze and food faster than the unfortunate host can say 'where the hell have all my vol-au-vents gone?' The media whore will turn up to anything and ask for everything. Then when it's time to go home they expect a goodie bag stocked full of expensive treats, a free cab home and maybe even some kind of sexual favour.

Socialite / Supermodel / Jobbing Actor / Pop Singer

Any job reliant on natural good looks and a vacancy of mind is top draw and the socialite-turned-model-turned-actress-turned-singer is a blagger *par excellence* amongst pikeys. By dint of good birth into the upper classes and/or attractive genes, the SSJP will wangle their way into numerous jobs which involve posing in front of a camera for a great deal of money, drinking at parties and sniffing coke off toilets seats more expensive than most people's houses. Scrimping on food bills ensures the pikey can squeeze into free designer garb and, once ensconced as pampered spouse to an older European aristocrat, their work is done.

Step 6: The Pikey in Middle Age

With middle age comes the power of knowledge, and by this stage the pikey is fully equipped to take advantage of the ignorance of others in a Jedi Mind Control style. This Pikey

Master also harnesses the added clout of accumulated riches, snaffled away over years of scrimping, which places them in a position of great influence and even greater potential pikey gain. But, like eating prawn vindaloo, there's always a downside and in this case it's the leaching spongers known as 'the family'.

It is now harder than ever for the Pikey Master to ride the crest of the wave, keeping outgoings lower than incomings, even if they've got so many loyalty card points they've been offered shares in various companies as a precautionary measure. Thus they must operate under the façade of Pikey Mentor, pretending to impart knowledge but really protecting their own interests: what's otherwise known as 'tough love'.

Constantly on the lookout to save resources, the Pikey Master rules with a rod of iron when it comes to conserving electricity and making phone calls before six. Fanatical in their quest to save a few pennies, they will drive for miles downhill to the cheapest petrol station before getting the kids to push the car home. At mealtimes the Pikey Master will regularly voice great concern for the starving children of Africa to prevent their children asking for seconds, but there is no evidence that they have ever actually contributed to this cause.

A strictly two-cups-from-one-teabag person, the Pikey Master regularly places the family in peril with their flagrant disregard for out-of-date food and can often be heard asserting that in their day there were no 'best before' dates. Other methods of indoctrination include instilling a strong sense of financial independence in their children, i.e. taking their paper-round money for rent, and encouraging atheism as a means of avoiding monetary outlay at Christmas.

The Pikey Master is distinguished by an exceptionally cutting-edge taste in clothes, but this is completely unintentional and has only happened as a result of the cyclical nature of fashion. This fluke adds untold value to all of the crap they've hoarded since childhood and the Pikey Master can often be spotted in the background of *The Antiques Roadshow* with their loot safely stowed away in an armour-plated van.

Step 7: The Pikey Rides Again

When life has run its course and the pensionable age has struck, the elderly pikey isn't the type to just sit back and wait to be shipped off to the knacker's yard. Far from it: being geriatric affords the Pikey Duffer the opportunity to go the full circle back to childlike dependency, to sit back, relax and feign memory loss whilst guilt-tripping those around them into tending to their every need. This works perfectly in tandem with a pension and all of the discounts available to them – free bus travel, false teeth and glasses – to make these twilight years the transcendent stage in the life of a pikey.

Equating Meals-on-Wheels with dinner at the Ritz, the Pikey Duffer instead survives on tinned food kindly donated by local school children at Christmas. Pilchards, sardines, corned beef, prunes and semolina are all part of their non-perishable diet which only lapses down the day centre when they are offered a pink wafer biscuit or some blancmange.

Cashing in their chips from a lifetime of supporting their

children, the Pikey Duffer won't have to pay a penny towards their plush accommodation in a nice home when the time comes and in fact makes positive moves towards being re-housed. For a long time they are unable to get used to having the heating on for more than one hour and automatically put cling film on the windows, their answer to double-glazing, until it sinks in that it's not them who're paying the bills so it doesn't matter.

Before shuffling off this mortal coil, the Pikey Duffer must shed all monetary and material assets (and redeem all their vouchers) in one final flourish of frivolity. Utilising a life-time's air miles they circumnavigate the globe four times and spend every winter in the Maldives. But of course they'll pretend they've said Margate and it just sounded funny because they didn't have their teeth in.

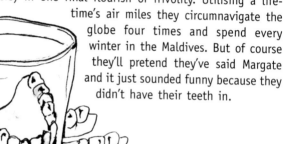

Pikey Hotspots

Pikey is all around. If you don't believe us have a gander at our beautifully produced map and marvel at the array of pikey attractions that litter our green and pleasant land. Then make a list, put your boots on, fill up the Thermos and jolly well get out there and enjoy yourself. Pikey is where you find it and that's pretty much everywhere in the UK, so there's no excuse not to seek out these hubs of pikey activity and get a piece of the action.

.99p

1 = London	The London Eye. Britain's celebration of the coming of a new millennium – a giant ferris wheel
2 = Margate	Chas 'n' Dave country and caravan central
3 = Blackpool	Poor man's Vegas
4 = Southend	Poor man's Blackpool
5 = Peckham	Birthplace of Del Trotter
6 = Lowestoft	Pleasurewood Hills. Poor man's Alton Towers, which is in turn the poor man's Disneyland
7 = Norwich	Trishatown
8 = Hartlepool	Home of Britain's only off-shore, tax-free off licence
9 = Dover	Destination booze cruise
10 = Dunsilly	Ireland's largest boot sale
11 = Ireland	Tax-free haven for writers
12 = Crumlin, Wales	Pot Noodle factory
13 = Wimbledon Common	Wombleland
14 = Oxon	Bicester Village. International outlet shopping village
15 = Manchester	Home of the Royle family
16 = Yorkshire	Home of Asda
17 = North Weald	Largest Saturday market in the UK
18 = Catterick	The largest Sunday market in the North of England
19 = Skegness	Europe's largest 7-day market – the Eastgate 7-day Market
20 = Glasgow	Barra Market
21 = Skipton	Charity shop capital of the North
22 = Otley	Also charity shop capital of the North – controversial
23 = Chigwell	Home of the Essex Girl
24 = Liverpool	Home of bread-eating Scousers
25 = Holmfirth	Compo town

SPECIAL OFFER !!

£0.00

CRAZY SAVINGS!

The Pikey
at Play

A pikey's home is his castle. The pikey will only venture out of the house when strictly necessary, for instance when Lulu's opening a new Weigh 'n' Save down the local precinct. Otherwise they'll follow the hibernation pattern of the *Blue Peter* tortoise. Though it may look like an utter dump from the outside, the home is the epicentre of the pikey's life, a refuge from the world where they can enjoy the fruits of their labour without spending a single penny.

.99p

In selecting the ultimate property, the pikey has factored in such crucial requirements as:

- low council tax
- accessibility to local charity and catalogue shops
- conveniently positioned street lighting to save on electricity bills
- room on the drive for a caravan

Pikeys usually keep the outside of their abode in a state of disrepair to deter any prospective burglars or friends. All visitors, should they be lucky enough to make it through the Fort Knox home security into the hallway, will be asked immediately to remove any footwear for fear of wearing out the plastic sheeting that covers the colourful disarray of carpet sample tiles adorning the floor. Hats and coats will be whisked off to a 'cloakroom' and not returned, while guests are distracted by the offer of a cup of tea and a biscuit, which will undoubtedly never materialise.

Stepping into the kitchen is akin to entering the land of giants. Dwarfed by catering-sized jars of pickled eggs and gherkins, vats of economy baked beans and skip-fulls of rice, there is no chance of starving should the much-anticipated millennium bug ever happen. There's never a dull meal in the pikey house; with a cornucopia of dented and label-less tins to choose from, it's not so much a lucky dip as a challenge to the constitution. At the forefront of fusion cookery, the pikey will not baulk at teaming pilchards with rice pudding.

A staggering array of kitchen gadgets picked up at boot sales poses massive health and safety risks for the neighbourhood as the pikey pursues their ongoing dream of inventing the world's first fully automated fry-up machine. Dinner is served on a collection of mismatched crockery and glassware liberated from pubs and service stations nationwide. On rare celebratory occasions, it has been known for the pikey to whip up some home-made champagne by giving a bottle of Blue Nun the SodaStream treatment.

A triumph of bad taste, the pikey living room is a homage to *Changing Rooms*. Never one to miss a trick, pikeys creatively plaster their walls with a lurid collage of wallpaper samples, juxtaposing 1980s bachelor pad with Indian restaurant flock to dramatic effect. In accordance with the latest phase of the Pikey School of Interiors, a love of budget airlines is reflected in the pikey's choice of armchairs with fold-out TV dinner tables, antimacassars and footrests. Pikeys amass a vast library of taped-from-TV films, all meticulously catalogued in old school exercise books and precariously stacked on shelves made from bricks and planks salvaged from a local building site.

No pikey living room would be complete without two obligatory items: the globe-shaped paper lampshade and pub-sized whisky bottles filled to capacity with coppers and French francs. When times are even harder, the pikey will spend literally hours counting out his shrapnel into small plastic bags so as not to be conned by the new-fangled change machine in their local supermarket.

Sleep is cheap and one of the pikey's favourite ways of economising, making the bedroom their little nest of sloth. Catching more z's than Rip Van Winkle, kipping on a cheap futon is their favourite way of staying warm and spending no money. Should one venture into the bedroom, perhaps to take a tumble with an amorous pikey, be sure to take advantage of one of the few surviving Teasmade in the country.

The bathroom, should one need a tinkle or a wash whilst round the pikey house, is a triumph of practicality over hygiene. Not only will they flush the toilet one in every five uses, but with a brick in the cistern to conserve water it's probably best if you can hold on. The sink is adorned with an array of soaps that the pikey has hoarded from B&Bs, bars

and Christmas crackers. Scraps too small to use will make it into the soap mould, that beautiful implement bought from the Innovations catalogue which allows the pikey to reshape old soaps into spanking new bars. A black line drawn in indelible ink around the bath determines how far one is allowed to fill the tub, a rule that must be strictly adhered to. Always in the vanguard of kitsch chic, pikeys just love a stunning toilet roll dolly, knitted by granny, to add a touch of class to the proceedings.

For a breath of fresh air, step out into the garden and have a seat on the park bench or just move the patio furniture out of the living room and sit on that. The pikey has no aesthetic ideals when it comes to the great outdoors and has little comprehension of landscape gardening, opting instead to turn the whole thing into a giant vegetable patch. Rows upon rows of root vegetables as well as a few illegal herbs and a giant beanstalk all grow in perfect harmony, together with the pikey's unsuccessful experiments in genetically engineering a real money tree.

Cheap as Chips:
CHEAP! The Ultimate Pikey Dinner Party

It's inevitable that after dining out round friends' houses time and again the spotlight is turned on the pikey to provide a night of sustenance and entertainment. Under duress, the pikey can muster up a cheap feast that will satiate the most eager of appetites and, most importantly, placate so-called chums who were considering withholding further invitations round their place for tea. Should you find yourself in such an unenviable situation as this, we have just the solution: a five-course dinner for four that comes in at under £10. These recipes are particular favourites of ours and have left many friends green with envy. What better recommendation than that?

.99P

Chilled Lambrusco and Home-made Bombay Mix

1 x 100g packet of mild curry
  Super Noodles
50g dried peas
1 x 75cl bottle of Lambrusco
  Bianco

Place Super Noodles in a plastic bag and bash with rolling pin. Decant into a serving bowl, mix in the dried peas and season with the sachet of dried flavour powder from the noodles. Accompany with a chilled glass of wine.

Cost: 56p per person

Starter

Exquisite Crab Paste Mousse with Toast

2 x 75g pots of crab paste
200g full-fat soft cheese
Squeeze of lemon
Black pepper
4 slices of white bread
Parsley garnish

Empty the crab paste into a bowl, being sure to eek out every remnant. Likewise for the cream cheese. Gently combine into a fluffy paste, adding a squeeze of lemon and just a grind or two of black pepper. Cut the crusts off the bread and whack it in the toaster. When toasted, cut into four fingers per slice. Serve one spoonful of mousse per guest on a side plate with the toast fingers artfully arranged beside it. Garnish with parsley.

Cost: 55p per serving

Main Course

Spajitas

> 1 x 340g tin of Spam
> 2 x red peppers
> 1 onion
> Garlic powder
> Chilli powder
> Dried mixed herbs
> Seasoning
> Another squeeze of lemon
> 1 packet of 8 flour tortillas
> Vegetable oil
> Parsley garnish

Prepare the Spam by cutting the block into long strips. Finely slice the onion and slice the peppers. Heat some oil in a pan and gently fry the Spam and vegetables until they begin to colour. Add as much garlic powder, chilli powder, herbs, lemon and seasoning as it takes to mask the taste. Serve with heated tortillas. Garnish with parsley.

Cost: 75p per serving

✳ Afters

Mini Tinned Fruit Pavlovas with Tip Top

*1 x 411g tin of fruit
   cocktail in syrup*
4 meringue nests
1 x 165g tin of Tip Top
Parsley garnish

Arrange the fruit salad inside the meringue nest and top off with Tip Top. Garnish with parsley.

Cost: 26p per serving

✳ Coffee and Delicious Home-made Chocolate Mint Crisps

200g dark chocolate
1 packet of mint tic tacs

Crush the tic tacs in a bag using a rolling pin. Melt the chocolate in the microwave. Combine the chocolate and crushed mints. Pour the mixture into a large baking tray lined with tin foil and place in the fridge to set. When solid, cut into squares. Serve with black instant coffee.

Cost: 16p per serving

After-Dinner Games

Der-Plonk

Take a cheese grater and insert cocktail
sticks through the holes and out the other
side. Drop glacé cherries on top of the
sticks and have a competition to see who
can remove the most sticks without the
cherries falling through. Two to four
players.

Who Could It Be?

Cut pictures of your favourite pikey celebrities from
doctor's surgery magazines and use your work's photo-
copier to make two duplicates of each picture. Back
with card nicked from the stationery cupboard. Lay a
set of celebrities out in front of each player and ask
each player to select a celebrity from the third set of
cards. Players then take turns to identify the mystery
celebrity by asking such questions as 'Is she missing
her septum? Does she have a trout pout?' The winner
is the first person to correctly deduce the other's
celebrity.

Join 4

A whimsical little game for two players that can be
played before, during or after dinner. Using a potato
waffle as a 'grid', players select their counters of choice,

usually peas or beans, and take it in turns to insert said counters into the 'gaps' in the waffle. The first player to complete a horizontal, vertical or diagonal line of four consecutive 'counters' may declare themselves the winner.

Medical Procedure!

A game requiring an incredibly steady hand. Players pick out crumbs from a plugged-in toaster using a pair of metal tweezers, the object of the game being to avoid electrocuting oneself.

Bender

Test your balance and flexibility and get the party going by pulling back a strategically placed rug to reveal coloured circles painted on the floor. One player then directs the others to place their hands and feet on various colours, for example, 'Left hand, Homebase green, right hand, road-marking yellow.' The aim of the game is to be the last player standing. Hilarious fun for all the family.

Pastimes

Being the finely tuned instruments of frugality that they are, pikeys have no time in their busy schedules for frittering away cash on hobbies. Learning to ride a horse, play the piano, or putt a golf ball into a tiny hole may well result in a well-rounded personality and great dinner-party conversation, but what use is that when you're dead and buried? Any spare moments in the day not spent soaking lentils or thinking up inventions on the loo must be given over to the pursuit of pleasure and profitability – that's two treats in one, both beginning with p.

.99p

Bingo

Bingo was invented in the 1530s by the Italians, who tagged it *'Lo Giuoco del Lotto D'Italia'*. Name us a man who's ever called his dog that. The craze soon swept through the French upper classes while the ever-efficient Germans used it as an educational tool (yawn) and the Americans played it with beans as counters. But it was the Brits who made it their own with rhyming slang, giant felt-tip pens and compulsively gambling blue-rinsed grannies. Bingo offers a night of entertainment, food, drink, and even cabaret, along with the chance of winning up to £200,000. Not even Armageddon could keep the pikeys away. By that we mean the end of the world, not the film.

Bingo facts

Celebrity fans include Kate Moss and Sadie Frost, Elizabeth Hurley and Russell Crowe – Robbie Williams has even been spotted pouring his heart out to a granny at bingo in Stoke.

Catherine Zeta-Jones has crossed new frontiers in her quest to take bingo to Hollywood and has been known to whip out a bingo set at the end of her star-studded parties. She puts on a bingo session every Christmas and on one occasion hubbie Michael even won a nice bottle of aftershave.

Some pikey bingo calls, coming to a hall near you:

Ford Capri = 3
Bailiffs at the door = 24
3 for 2 = 32
Spam for tea = 43

Car Boot Sales

Any pikey worth their salt will be up at the crack of dawn on a Saturday morning to elbow their way to the front of the boot sale queue. The keenest amongst them will rummage through the contents of another's car boot before the owner's even left their house. Boot sales came into popularity during the recession when people would try to scrape a few pennies together by selling off their unwanted possessions or annoying relatives, but their popularity has hardly diminished since. There's nothing available in the shops that won't be going for a song at a boot sale.

Ten items indubitably found at every boot sale

* Prints from Athena, like that one of the man holding the baby
* Old cuddly toys covered in other people's dribble marks
* Faded, unused toiletry sets containing rose-scented talc and bath pearls
* Workout videos from the eighties – Cindy Crawford, Mr Motivator *et al.*
* Old Happy Meal toys
* Stock, Aiken and Waterman tapes
* Haynes car manual for cars that are so old they can only be found in Cuba
* Old hamster cages and fish bowls from long-forgotten pets
* Stonewashed denim with patches and/or paint splattering
* Grotty recorders with teeth marks on the mouthpiece

✳ Complaining

While pikeys are distinguished by a certain *joie de vivre* and upbeat attitude towards life, they are not unfamiliar with the effectiveness of a good complaint. In fact for some it's a fine art worthy of many hours of tireless application. A seasoned complainer videotapes *Watchdog* religiously and commits it to memory, often seeking out offending companies and corporations as targets for their next hit. The complainer knows their consumer rights like the back of their hand and is not embarrassed to ask for a full refund, compensation and a letter of apology from a charity shop selling shirts with buttons missing.

How To Complain

* Complaining involves strategy, tactics, psychological trickery, undermining an opponent, pitting your wits and pitching in for a battle. A short stint in the TA will hone all of these skills.
* Keep a diary of everything that goes wrong with a product or service so that you have a barrage of ammo for when they try to weasel their way out of giving you a refund.
* Find a contact within the company you are complaining to and then email them, phone them, fax them, write them countless letters, send dolls with their heads hacked off to their children and sit outside their house wearing night-vision goggles.
* Complaining is like bartering – if you ask for what you want then you will end up with less. Start with outrageous requests for compensation, claim that you have been mentally affected by the experience and need a house in Barbados to recover and see what you can get.
* Coffee that is hot, burgers that make you fat, flies

in soup – forget that this is normal and feign utter ignorance to get compensation for things being exactly as they should be. Stupidity can be your best tool.

DIY

Great Britain is a veritable hub of DIY activity. Us pikey Brits adore nothing more than an over-ambitious home improvement project and will gladly spend an entire weekend trailing round B&Q looking for the right kind of rawlplug or a flat-pack conservatory complete with decking, barbecue and mini-bar that will make the neighbours weep with jealousy. Never mind the fact that we spend over £850m a year calling out the professionals to put right the errors of our ways, the average DIY fanatic sees himself as a regular Handy Andy, regardless of the consequences . . .

Perils of pikeyness

* 70 people are killed and 250,000 people injured every year in DIY-related accidents. Of these, 100,000 are injured seriously enough to warrant a visit to casualty.
* 40,000 DIY accidents a year involve stepladders.

* In 1999 1,400 people injured themselves over the Easter break. It was the most dangerous period of the year with 200,000 DIY-related injuries and 70 deaths.
* People aged 30 to 39 are most at risk of injuring themselves in the course of improving their home. They are most likely to tackle complex jobs beyond their handyman capabilities and least likely to wear safety gear or ask for advice.

eBaying

Cruising the information superhighway has become *de rigueur* amongst those seeking to be a thoroughly modern pikey and eBay is the perfect place to incubate and implement many ways of saving and making cash. The owners of this site have opened up free trade between pikeys all over the world. Not only are there many bargains to be had but half the pleasure is thinking up persuasive sales pitches to sell old crap that you would otherwise chuck out.

eBay facts

* When Tesco launched a £45 version of a £1,400 green Chloé dress sported by Kylie, wily pikeys sold them online for up to £75.

* The *Mirror* decided to hoax gullible shoppers on the site by listing fake items from various celebrities. Wayne Rooney's old pizza box, an empty whisky bottle from Britney Spears' hotel room, MRSA and Jesse Wallace's old tissue all featured on the site and each received bids. True pikeys weren't taken in.
* Cherie Blair blagged a £20 children's clock for 99p in an eBay auction for her son Leo. She earns over £250,000 a year as a barrister and public speaker but made a bid at the minimum sum. She even invited the seller round for a cup of tea at Number 10, presumably so she'd save on postage.

Going to the Pub

Going to the pub is by far the most popular pastime for natives of the British Isles, who like nothing more than to evade life's problems by prevaricating over a pint. Though it can be a costly business, going to the boozer needn't be out of bounds for the pikey-minded as it is certainly possible that the customs, rituals and traditions of pub-going can be bent to suit the needs of those on a budget. Becoming a regular at your local by befriending the landlord, flirting with the old men at the bar and having in-depth philosophical debates with the local drunkard is a pre-requisite to pikey pub-going. The pikey lush selects a local with care, as it's their hallowed turf and a home from home with free electricity, heating, and cable television.

Pikey Pub Protocol

* Go through all the dramatic motions of having lost your wallet, knowing full well you've left it at home.
* Choose a pub that welcomes dealers in contraband designer clothing, fags and knocked-off DVDs (all strictly kosher despite being sold from the boot of a Capri) so that you can pick up a few bargains while you're there.
* Clock up unlimited hours of pool playing by cunningly secreting beer mats in the pockets of the pool table.
* Take a leaf out of the pensioners' book and become a potman – collecting glasses and wiping tables all day in return for free pints is better than getting a proper job.
* Become the local darts champ. Invest in a shell suit and some cheap bling *à la* Bobby George and take full advantage of the free sausage sangers and chips in a basket during amateur tournaments. Let's . . . play . . . darts!!!
* Make use of your dressed-down boho style to get into student bars. Pick up a couple of philosophy books from the charity shop and tuck them under your arm to lend a touch of authenticity.
* Work out the longest-playing songs on the jukebox. Anything by Meatloaf, Dire Straits or Lynyrd Skynyrd is guaranteed to offer value for money.

Impersonating Celebrities

If you had the misfortune to grow up to look like Ken Dodd it need not be the end of the world. By whoring your soul and pretending to be someone else until it eclipses your own personality you can become a celebrity look-alike and enjoy all kinds of fringe benefits – an appearance on *Stars in their Eyes* is the first rung on the ladder to opening local supermarkets and blagging free champagne in the Met Bar. Even the likes of Ian McShane, Claire Sweeney and John Virgo have pikey alter egos who will turn up to the opening of a bean can given the chance. It's easier than you think to pass yourself off as a celebrity; don't let a small thing like being white get in the way of impersonating Linford Christie; it's all about having the right tracksuit.

Metal Detecting

Metal detecting is one of the most misunderstood of the pikey pleasure pursuits. To the untrained eye the metal detectorist cuts a lonesome figure, scouring the British coastline in the hope of finding someone's old Elizabeth Duke earring. But he knows that cavorting in the sea can also result in losing an expensive diamond ring. A few days out with the metal detector and the pikey can amass

obscene amounts of loot, which can then be smelted down to make a giant golden palace with diamond chandeliers and a ruby-encrusted koi carp pond. Or sold on eBay.

✳ Puzzling

The obsessive-compulsive of the pikey world, the puzzler can simultaneously complete *The Sunday Times* crossword whilst committing *The Guinness Book of Records* to memory and thrashing the whole family at Trivial Pursuit. Once they've fitted their numerous prize cars and washing machines into the garage there's barely any room for the year's supply of cat food and beer, never mind the fact that they're feline-hating teetotallers. Intolerable bores to those who are not members of their pub quiz team, they are distinguished by a unique speech impediment: the need to finish every sentence in twenty-five words or less . . .

The Pikey on TV

If there's one pastime that's kept the pikey occupied throughout recent history it's sitting goggle-eyed in front of the television. Quite what pikeys did before the invention of the telly is unknown, though we are led to believe they just stared at the wall. As well as being cheap, on-tap all day and night, and involving little physical exertion, watching television is prime research material for living the pikey lifestyle. The British have been weaned on programmes that celebrate the resourcefulness and downright beauty of those living on slender means. We wouldn't call it brainwashing as such, but the triumph of the underdog and the promotion of thriftiness that permeate the television diet of the average Brit has made a definite contribution towards the popularity of pikeyness today.

.99p

Blue Peter

Blue Peter has been around since before the beginning of time divulging all kinds of resourceful tips to the young and easily swayed. Thanks to them, the nation's youth is fully equipped to make fifty different functional household items from an empty cereal box and can fashion a replica Tracy Island from four toilet rolls and a used *Heat* magazine.

Steptoe & Son

Purveyors of the sadly diminishing rag-and-bone trade, this father and son duo made a living by collecting other people's tat in their Shepherd's Bush junkyard and trying very unsuccessfully to sell it. Though their house was a dump, they had terrible clothes, rotting teeth, and were desperately unhappy, their sheer determination to remain pikey gives them a place in our hearts. Although the old one's so ugly it's hard to look at him.

The Wombles

Pikeyness has never been so cute. The little Wombles, wombling around Wimbledon Common, were like a better-looking, more polite version of *Steptoe & Son* and turned a whole generation of kids' TV viewers into pikey scavengers. The ultimate recyclers, they collected litter that everyday people left behind and crafted it into indispensable gadgets such as string telephones and conker abacuses. Bless 'em.

Worzel Gummidge

As well as being utterly terrifying, Worzel Gummidge was one of the chief pikey progenitors of his time. Firstly he was made of straw and old clothes. Secondly, he would scare people into giving him 'a cup o' tea an' a nice slice o' cake'. Thirdly he would steal anything that wasn't nailed down, including furniture and freshly washed pants. Fourthly, he listed Babs Windsor amongst his friends. Enough said? Well, no, for at one point Worzel even made it to New Zealand. Never mind how he paid the fare, how the hell did he get through customs?

Dad's Army

Britain's last line of defence against Nazi invasion, this ragtag bunch of Home Guard volunteers demonstrated how pikeyness thrived *in extremis*. And, of course, the series paid homage to that great figure of wartime entrepreneurialism: the spiv. Private Walker was a cockney with his eye on the prize who laughed in the face of wartime cutbacks and rationing, and could lay his hands on anything from a sniffer dog to a pair of stockings. When he wasn't committing blackmail, he would steal the pigeons from Trafalgar Square and flog them to the local butcher, or smuggle Italian POW's out of the camp to work in a factory. In short, he was a genius.

Bagpuss

Bagpuss was a fat cat, and if that's not heavy-handed symbolism then we don't know what is. Rather than the lazy pink feline he's misconstrued to be, Bagpuss was a tremendous business-cat. For the proportion of the day he was actually awake, he was head honcho at the 'shop for found things' – an ostensibly charitable operation which reunited people with things they had lost, but one which miraculously managed to pay the rent. Ever the corporate bigwig, Bagpuss was savvy enough to employ an entire army of rodent proletarians, mice whose every waking hour was dictated by 'The Pink One'. Innocent childhood entertainment this certainly was not. Now hands up who tried to make one of those chocolate biscuit mills . . .

3–2–1

Not only was the show's concept stolen from the Spanish programme *Un, Dos, Tres* but *3–2–1* ran on the Kinder Egg principle: a quiz, variety show and game show in one, and its quantity never compensated for its lack of quality. In a masterstroke of nonsensical quizmanship, ex-Butlins red-coat Ted Rogers would fire impossibly cryptic clues to intellectually stunted couples from the West Midlands who nonetheless had more brain cells between them than an entire *Family Fortunes* team put together. No self-respecting child of the eighties could ever work out why Dusty Bin was considered the booby prize, given that he was a technological marvel on roller skates powered by four AA batteries who came with a whole range of comedy outfits.

☀ Dr Who

In its early years the show with possibly the most conspicuously low production values ever known was not only a genius of pikey television-making, but *Dr Who* thoroughly espoused its own values. At the core of the programme lies not the ever-changing figure of the Dr himself but rather his mode of transport and accommodation: the Tardis, a pikey des res beyond compare. A veritable mansion hidden within a  police box, the Tardis embodies everything the ideal portable home should be – it occupies a low land-rent bracket, is spacious, travels with ease through the space-time continuum, never needs petrol and can disappear on cue. And it's nicked. From the police.

☀ Bullseye

In a bold leap for the game-show format, *Bullseye* combined favourite British pub-based pastimes, the pub quiz and darts, featuring a team of two friends, one good at general knowledge, the other good at darts. Primitive sunbeds and lawnmowers were regular prizes on the show, where ultimately players could gamble their winnings for the *pièce de résistance* – usually a speedboat that would inevitably end up on bricks in the winner's back garden in Corby. Losers would be given a packet of darts and a Bendy Bully or, even worse, be shown what they could have won and sent away with their BFH – bus fare home.

☆ Button Moon

Button Moon was the height of low-budget chic and its star, Mr Spoon, was made of (wait for it) spoons. Never one to let his humble cooking implement origins get in his way, Mr Spoon was a pioneer of pikey space travel and managed to get from A to B inside a spaceship made from a baked bean can. That's amazing, although what he was doing with such a large can of beans when he was so small is quite puzzling. Perhaps he had an intergalactic Cash 'n' Carry card?

☆ Only Fools and Horses

With a theme tune that may as well be a pikey call-to-arms, *Only Fools* is the prime example of pikeyness in the mainstream and we just lapped it up. Del Trotter (Del Boy to his accomplices) is Peckham's very own King of Bling and the epitome of the cockney wide-boy on the make. He took wheeling and dealing to dizzying new heights in his quest to live the high life at low cost, selling all kinds of tat to unsuspecting pikeys who thought they were getting a bargain. He also cultivated a unique glamorous pikey style with his beautiful golden jewellery and penchant for cocktails with sparklers in them. Even the Queen is a fan. Pikey.

Bread

Set in Scouseland during the recession, *Bread* featured the dysfunctional Boswells, a family that made Jeffrey Archer look like Mother Theresa. Keeping it in the family, they pooled their resources in Ma Boswell's chicken-shaped pot, collectively screwing over the benefit system whilst working on the side. Family trips to the DHSS office happened on a weekly basis, where leather-clad charmer Joey still managed to blag his money off the stoney-faced Martina, who disregarded the fact he was the only man in Liverpool with a car not up on bricks (let alone the fact it was a Jag) and one of the first scousers to own a mobile phone. Greetings!

Lovejoy

The leather jacket, the mullet; we're clearly in the presence of Pikey royalty. Who other than Britain's best-loved antiques dealer? Lovejoy lived hand-to-mouth but was always ready to pull a fast one. His droopy-eyed charm got him into many a scrape (well, as many as there are to be had in the musty antiques business) but our big-haired pal always managed to extricate himself from a dodgy situation and land himself a bit of an antique bargain in the process. No, we're not talking about Joanna Lumley.

Shameless

Just when the spate of ultra-glam series like *Sex and the City* and *Footballers' Wives* (programmes that espoused the values of being rich, having too many shoes and having a fountain in your front garden) seemed to have killed off the pikey on TV, *Shameless* came along and put everything right. Seeing the Gallagher family live out their life of scams is like watching all the pikey energy that's been incubating over the past ten years let out in one glorious, joyous outburst. A true pikey would rather have a tinnie on the sofa with Frank than a cocktail with Carrie Bradshaw any day.

✳ Reality TV: the Pikey Take-over

With the dawn of the nineties came the invention of reality television. Every pikey producer's dream, it gave television-makers the chance to save a fortune by replacing sitcoms and expensive actors with real-life muppets who would shamelessly display their innate lack of personality to the viewing nation for a moment of fame. It didn't take long before every facet of television's rich intellectual output was commandeered by a reality show – from home improvements to fashion, cookery, singing and even rummaging through the jumble sale, there was nothing a professional could do that a pleb pulled off the streets couldn't do just as well. Or so they thought. While *Bootsale Challenge*, *Bargain Hunt*, *Cash in the Attic* and their ilk are high up on the pikey's viewing agenda, is another stint of reality game shows strictly necessary? When living in fear of being caught without a television licence, the pikey demands something decent to watch.

As digital television opens up avenues for entertainment that would never find its way onto terrestrial television, an increasing number of specialist channels have materialised, each staking a claim on their little corner of the market. Imagine our surprise when one of our media moles came to us with plans for PTV: an all-new station chock-full of pikey programming. This should be right up our street, only a quick glance at their listings and we get the feeling we've seen it all before . . .

PTV: the No-Frills Broadcasting Corporation

9.00 Tanya

Our sparky host Tanya, who's been through the mill in this life, she can tell you, invites guests onto the show to talk over dilemmas such as whether to marry an abusive alcoholic or confess to how they went out and got shitfaced one night and woke up pregnant. Tanya intervenes with her most patronising and obvious advice, which the guests (whose coffee was spiked with a sedative before they came on stage) greet with slack-jawed subjugation. Filmed on location in Ipswich.

10.00 Changing Rooms: The Revenge

The tables are turned on celebrity interior designers when they return from holiday to find that past recipients of their hideous home make-overs have redecorated their houses with obnoxiously coloured paints and cheap fabrics. This week the embittered Petersons from Doncaster install a highly flammable kitchen entirely constructed from laminated shoe boxes in Carol Smilie's home. Repeat.

13.00 Washed-up Women

Female celebrity has-beens give more shitty anecdotes about their shitty lives in an attempt to validate their existence and stay off the dole.

15.00 Daylight Robbery

New programming for a previously untapped daytime audience giving guidance on how to rob the vacant houses of those unlucky enough to be out at work. Tips on how to case a joint are followed by live-action footage as one of our volunteers actually commits a robbery, after which a brightly spectacled host is on hand to give indispensable tips on where to flog their new red-hot loot.

16.00 Jelly-Flubbies

Four out-of-work actors stumble around in coloured fat suits on a cheapo wobbly set yelling out baby-voiced gibberish.

18.30 Ready, Steady, Miracle!

Brand new reality television show in which eight of the country's finest television chefs are given two days, two fish and five loaves of bread and, whilst being filmed from every possible angle, are set the task of making a meal for five thousand.

19.00 Bone Idol

More lacklustre reality television in which Simon Cowell wrings even more money out of his single ropey game show concept by conducting a search for the nation's pikiest person. Reusing the Big Brother *house once again, this no-frills production will pit idler against idler in a game of benefit fraud, wheeling and dealing, and effort-free living. The winner receives none of Cowell's substantial profits but is nonetheless content to have lived for free for twelve weeks and needs to be forcibly evicted.*

20.00 Billy Idol

More lacklustre reality television in which Simon Cowell wrings even more money out of his single ropey game show concept by conducting a search for the nation's most convincing Billy Idol imper-sonator. Repeated on Sundays with the accompanying documentary You're Too Fat to be Famous *in which viewers are invited to ridicule the overweight people who had the cheek to enter a public competition.*

21.00 Dad, You're a Wanker

Working-class dads attempt utterly impossible challenges to win the prizes of a lifetime for their family, only to be humiliated in front of the nation and rejected by their snivelling, ungrateful spawn. This week Dave, a blind father of four, has two days in which to commit Tchaikovsky's Piano Concerto No. 2 to memory and perform it flawlessly with the Royal Philharmonic Orchestra in the Albert Hall.

22.30 I Love . . . I Love . . . Everything!

More glassy-eyed reminiscences from celebrity morons who, in a desperate bid to save their careers, have given themselves over to rounds of mind-numbing punditry in the unsubstantiated belief that their opinions will strike a chord with the viewing public and they'll be welcomed back onto the telly with warm hearts and open arms.

23.00 Who Wants to be a Legionaire?

A group of ten young offenders are given the chance to dodge prison by volunteering for the French Foreign Legion. What the producers don't realise is that once they've left the country and changed their names, they'll run for the hills quicker than you can say 'penal code'.

Top of the Shops

The pikey code of honour stipulates that you should never ever pay full price for anything. Combating consumerism by never taking anything at face value, the pikey will go to ridiculous lengths to swindle the shops for the sake of paying the lowest price for their purchases. The pikey would never be afraid to hold up a queue in order to count out over two years' worth of coppers for some bargain designer tracksuit bottoms in TK Maxx. Here we are delighted to share with you some trusty cut-price dependables.

☀ Charity Shops

Charity shopping involves a certain amount of application, dedication and sheer nerve in order to reap the rewards of flogging things on eBay for five times the price you paid for them. The only pitfall is the increase in stealth grannies who nab a voluntary job at the local Sue Ryder and then moonlight as a dealer in collectable china and rare first editions to top up their winter fuel allowance. One way of bypassing them is to volunteer at the charity shop yourself, or at the least work out the patterns of stock replenishment in order to have first dibs at the bargains. Alternatively move to Merseyside and catch one of the regular chartered coach trips to Skipton or Otley, two towns vying for the coveted title of 'charity shop capital of the North'. Or, now we come to think of it, just move to Skipton or Otley.

☀ Cash converters / Reclamation Centres / Pawnbrokers

There's no time for sentiment in the hard-edged world of pikey, so a quick trip down the reclamation centre to see what the bailiffs have managed to prise from the hands of the insolvent is always worth the effort. Pawnbrokers and Cash converters are also a great source of drastically undersold engagement rings and televisions. It's even worth suggesting to cash-strapped friends that pawning their shiny new widescreen telly is a good idea, just so you can nip in and bag it for fifty quid. Being soft will never get you anywhere.

Pound Shops

No respectable pikey can walk past a pound shop without at least having a peek, but crossing the threshold is the most lethal of decisions because once inside, it's impossible to resist the temptation of spending your very last tenner. You emerge ten minutes later with Christmas wrapping paper, 240 industrial-sized bin bags, scouring pads, a peg carousel, a garish eyeshadow set, a CD of orchestral Beatles covers, antifreeze, Chanel No.6 Eau de Toilette, a bumper set of felt-tip pens and a dancing sunflower bedecked with Roy Orbison shades. Penniless though you may be, there's no greater sense of achievement than returning home to parade your haul of tat in front of your senile granny.

High-Street Jewellers

If diamonds are a girl's best friend, then Elizabeth Duke is quite frankly her saviour. Bling can still be a part of the pikey's life even with its connotations of conspicuous consumption because of the Argos range of high quality, low price jewellery – or bling on a shoestring as it's commonly known. Lizzy D has provided almost every girl with her first pair of dolphin-shaped earrings and enables many a teenager to propose to his girlfriend with a cubic zircon ring. Otherwise it's over to Claire's Accessories for plenty of plastic on elastic, where you can see grown women fighting with eight-year-olds for the last pink glittery hair bobble.

Supermarket Clothes

Being able to pick up a bigger pair of trousers at the supermarket because you've been pigging out on BOGOFs is a great idea, and supermarket clothing lines are finding a place in the hearts of consumers who're happy to buy everything under one roof. Lord George of Asda is at the forefront of bringing cheap clothes and designer rip-offs to the masses, with Tesco coming up the rear with £4 jeans, dirt-cheap cashmere, and the infamous copy of Kylie's green Chloé dress.

Catalogue Shops

Where else in the world can you eagerly await the appearance of your number on a screen before seeing your prize roll off a giant conveyor belt? We're not talking about bingo or *The Generation Game* but the experience of shopping the catalogue way with Argos or Index. Forget *Vogue* and *GQ*, catalogues are the only consumer publications a pikey can flick through where the goods inside are actually attainable. It's a well-known fact that the pages of the in-store catalogues are laminated to protect them from pikey drool and that Argos's small blue biros crop up in the pencil cases of many a young pikelet. What's less apparent is the subculture of Argos bargain junkies whose dissemination of product codes is so effective that the sale's over before it's even begun.

Tantamount to having membership to the Groucho Club, a Cash 'n' Carry card is the ultimate status symbol amongst pikeys. Sudden popularity comes to every pikey in possession of a shiny new card, but the highly desirable guest pass should only be given to a friend with a van or, even better, access to a freight plane. Conversely, those without a card can spot a 'carrier' from the upside-down labels on their giant bottles of Czech spirits, bath-sized tubs of 'chef's' marge in their fridge and the fact that their salad cream comes in sachets. In this instance, they can be bribed into sharing the wealth, lest you shop them to the rest of the pikey community.

Tools of the Trade

Loyalty Cards

Points mean prizes and it's worth surrendering an Orwellian amount of deeply personal information about your consumer life patterns to the 'Nectar Card People' in order to amass enough credit for a free weekend in Champneys any day of the week. The loyalty card was invented by Tesco, but soon everyone wanted a piece of the action and now it's impossible for retailers to sell anything without giving customers a few pennies back for their troubles. But be warned: over-reliance on your loyalty card can seriously damage your health. Many an emaciated pikey has been found nibbling the edges of their Tesco Clubcard having let their cupboard run dry in anticipation of a double points day.

3-for-2s / BOGOFS / Multibuys

Ostensibly very much in the spirit of all things pikey, 3-for-2s and BOGOFs nevertheless require some investigation to discern their status as friend or foe to the conscientious pikey shopper. BOGOFs are clearly better value than 3-for-2s, but the latter has its place for certain non-perishable products which can be stowed away at home. Sharing a BOGOF with a friend is

very pikey indeed, but top draw every time has to be the multibuy favoured by Iceland, where it's possible to get a veritable medieval feast off the back of one packet of Findus Crispy Pancakes.

Sales

The best thing about Christmas is that every year the sales get earlier and earlier; even the Queen wants to ditch her speech so she can get down to Next for a few bargains. Queuing outside in sub-zero temperatures is essential if you're going to be first off the blocks when the doors open, and this is especially true when partaking in the Harrods sale. A British institution, this bargain bonanza prompts people who normally wouldn't be seen dead in posh areas to camp out in Knightsbridge, ready for a piece of the gigantic-reductions-on-luxurious-items action.

Can't Buy Me Love:
The Lost Art of Wooing

CHEAP!

With pikeyness becoming so popular these days, it's just too easy to take your beloved on a cheap weekend to Paris, obtain last-minute cut-price theatre tickets or save up coupons for a cheap meal at an Angus Steak House. But any pikey worth their salt knows these flashy romantic gestures are very tacky and anyone who's impressed by this isn't worth dating. If the spirit of pikeyness is to prevail in the dating arena then the little things that matter (i.e. the ones that don't cost much) need to be reinstated and celebrated. It's time for a wooing renaissance, for a return to the romantic touches that take thought, care and preparation. Think Romeo at Juliet's balcony. Think Sonny and Cher crooning 'I Got You Babe'. Think Frank Butcher standing at Pat's doorstep wearing naught but a rotating bowtie and a large smile. Speed dating is dead, long live wooing!

.99p

Cupboard love

Say it with . . . Alphabetti Spaghetti. There's no need to spend a fortune on a dozen roses to express your love when you can cook up a can of Alphabetti Spaghetti and write out your sentiments in pasta.

If music be the food of love

Make like Renee and Renato and serenade your lover with a heartfelt ballad. A couple of pints of snakebite and you'll be in fine voice to hit the karaoke machine with the chart-topping 'Save Your Love', performed with flamboyant gesticulation and a pained expression.

Pressing the right buttons

Think old skool. Homemade compilation tapes are a sure-fire way to show you've been paying attention to your sweetheart's declarations of love for Boney M, Wagner's 'Ring Cycle' and Girls Aloud. Those hours poised by the radio with your finger hovering over the record button may give you RSI but it'll be worth it.

Handbags and Gladrags

Pop to the charity shop and with a maximum of £10 pick each other a hideous outfit to wear that night at dinner in Maccie D's. It's two cheap dates in one, and a GSOH is priceless.

✴ Take Heart

Show your love exactly what you would buy for them if you were a cold-hearted consumerist by cutting pictures out of last year's Argos catalogue and making them a nice big collage to adorn their wall and remind them of you.

✴ A Boxcar Named Desire

Recreate the cosy intimacy of the drive-in in the comfort of your own living room by fashioning a 'lovebug' from a giant cardboard box, complete with frisbee steering wheel and foil quiche case headlights.

✴ Getting in-tents

Turn your back on the crowds and commercialism of modern music festivals by staging a private concert under the stars in your back garden. Pitch a tent, create a fire, stock up on cider and pretend that the acts are playing live and are not in fact booming from your lounge window. Randomly shout 'bollocks!' in the middle of the night, make your partner wait a minimum of twenty minutes for the loo and hide the toilet roll.

The Pikey Abroad

Gone are the days when the pikey would be content with a trip to Butlins or a rainy weekend in a caravan in Margate. Now that it's cheaper to fly abroad than it is to use the London Underground people are leaving the country in droves to spend their leisure time sapping Johnny Foreigner for all he is worth. Forgoing local culture, history and the chance of widening their horizons for the chance of living it up on the cheap for a couple of weeks, the pikey has a right royal time of it in a variety of exotic locations.

.99p

One of the biggest revolutions in pikey travel came with the low-budget airline which made travelling so cheap it's almost more expensive to stay at home. Pikeys love to fly no-frills and will book up to eight years in advance to get a return flight for 3p. They are not bothered about deep-vein thrombosis, four-day cross-continent coach transfers or flying via Timbuktu to Ireland. Once they have reached their target destination, pikeys will turn up unannounced on the doorstep of one of their many childhood pen pals or some long lost relative and expect to sleep in their bed and make love to their wife.

Alternatively, booking a last-minute package deal means the pikey need spend no more than the initial outlay for their holiday, as long they are prepared to live within the confines of a minimalist hotel for the duration of their stay. Feasting on the all-inclusive buffets they are like Mr T at a Ratners sale, but can't resist the urge to steal food for the intervening hours or raid the non-perishable condiments to take home to restock their larder. No matter how bad the in-house cabaret gets, the staunch pikey will be waving a lighter in the front row and will often start a conga line around the pool just for kicks.

The more adventurous pikey will end up miles beyond European borders, having hedged their bets on a £20 trip to India or Thailand which involves more hours on a leaky boat or atop a donkey than actual time on an aeroplane. But in their mind it is completely worth it, the joys of being able to live like a king on 50p a day far outweigh the physical torture of getting there. Many a savvy pikey has reached the shores of Asia by volunteering as an English teacher or eco-warrior, but the moment this seems too much like hard work has made a run for it and ended up having to swim back to Blighty or join a commune.

Regardless of their destination, one of the defining characteristics of the pikey abroad is their desperation to eek out every moment of their holiday. Rather than taking the time to wind down and recharge, the pikey goes for complete burnout and recuperates by taking sick days from work when they get home. That is, once they've sold all the duty-free cigarettes, bootleg DVDs, ethnic jewellery and illegal substances they've picked up on their travels to their workmates at a 'discount price'. In fact, anything that

can be bought on the cheap is safely stowed away in one of the pikey's many spare suitcases for later use.

ECIAL
OFFER !!

00.0ſ

CRAZY
SAVINGS!

The Pikey in Celebville

CHEAP!

Caught in the Act:
Celebrities at their Pikiest

Despite scaling the dizzy heights of fame, even the richest celebrity is not immune to the lure of being pikey. Most stars are fully aware that the trick to staying at the top lies in retaining those penny-pinching skills that smoothed the path from Basingstoke to Beverly Hills and that pretending to be 'down to earth' is a brilliant façade for being very tight. We've been sniffing around celebville and have unearthed some cunning celebrity ways of counting the pennies while the millions look after themselves.

.99p

1 Keep it real

Allegedly, for his wife Heather's birthday bash, millionaire Paul McCartney took a leaf out of his own songbook. Believing that 'money can't buy you love' saved the ex-Beatle a small fortune as he made all guests pay for their own drinks. Once a Scouser . . .

2 Don't be afraid to haggle

Apparently *Friends* star David Schwimmer threw a tantrum at a Hollywood restaurant after the manager refused to give him a discount on six bottles of champagne. Quite rightly, the £750,000-an-episode actor vowed never to set foot in the joint again. However, this still begs the question, had he not heard of Asti?

3 Argos is a girl's best friend

Canny diva Charlotte Church hasn't let fame go to her pretty little Welsh head. Mixing Chloé with clown pendants, she's a self-confessed fan of catalogue shop jewellery and wears replica bling when out on the town to avoid losing the real thing in the backs of cabs.

4 It's the thought that counts

Thoughtful rocker Mick Jagger knows

how to value his staff. While Elton John spends thousands on lavish gifts from Versace, Mick has been known to reward his entourage with a good old-fashioned potted plant.

5 Simple tastes

Turning her nose up at literally everything, Victoria Beckham is no different when it comes to fine wine. A connoisseur of all the truly indulgent things in life, its rumoured that she has crates of Blue Nun specially shipped to her Madrid mansion.

6 Dodge tax

It's the oldest celebrity trick in the book, accidentally 'forgetting' that the ordinary rules in life still apply to you in celebrity world. Coleen McLoughlin, sweetheart of England footballer Wayne Rooney, tried her hand at a spot of modern piracy but instead landed herself with a hefty tax bill after returning from New York with booty she hadn't paid duty on. There's a lesson to be learnt here: don't fly out in Kappa and return in Juicy Couture – you'll stick out like a sore thumb.

7 Live like the common people

Minnie Driver has turned her back on her privileged upbringing, swapping her Beverly Hills mansion for a Beverly Hillbillies-style caravan. According to Minnie, 'It's a nice trailer in a nice trailer park.' We'll keep an eye out for you on *Jerry*, Minnie.

8 Points mean prizes

Ever experienced the horror of arriving at the checkout only to discover you've forgotten your loyalty card? Its been reported that Angelina Jolie showed no shame in holding up the checkout queue whilst running back to retrieve her flexible friend and those precious points. She may be an internationally renowned film star but nothing will keep her from bagging those crystal wine glasses or a family day ticket to Alton Towers. Quite right.

9 Always check the bill

An eye-witness has claimed that thrifty Scot Rod Stewart made a 20-mile round trip back to an LA restaurant after being charged for a bottle of mineral water he hadn't ordered. Rod, worth a reputed £70 million, drove from his Beverly Hills mansion back to the swanky LA restaurant and refused to leave until the money was refunded to his credit card. Mr Stewart, we salute you, but hope you also billed them for petrol expenses.

Love for Sale:
The Rise of the
Celebrity Wedding

CHEAP!

Once a celebrity, why not continue to rake it in by joining in matrimony with a fellow pikey parasite? With pre-nuptials and later divorce settlements, the celebrity wedding is a regular cash cow and the good news is that the big bucks start rolling in with exclusive deals on the big day itself. Sell your soul to the devil but save a fortune on getting your wedding snaps printed and duplicated for friends by brokering a deal where every guest receives a free copy of *Hello!* magazine on publication. It would be a crime not to cash in.

.99p

✱ Catherine Zeta-Jones and Michael Douglas

Mr and Mrs Douglas won on both accounts with pay-outs from both *OK!* and *Hello!* magazines. The Welsh siren and her crinkly old man banked a staggering £1 million from *OK!* for exclusive pictures of their nuptials. But the former Darling Bud was not best pleased when she was papped looking far from her usual blooming self with her gob round a wedge of cake by a rogue *Hello!* snapper. The greedy couple demanded £600,000 from the cheeky mag for ruining their special, not to mention lucrative, deal, but they had to make do with a mere £14,600. CZ-J's pikey skills are second to none. She reportedly bags $2.8 million for every year of marriage. Wonder what she gets as a Christmas bonus?

✱ Anthea Turner and Grant Bovey

Golden TV girl Anthea's career literally crumbled in the marital aftermath that was Flakegate. The former *Blue Peter* presenter and her husband Grant Bovey gratefully accepted a whopping £300,000 from *OK!* to cover their wedding and blagged 500 free bars of chocolate from Cadbury as an extra little sweetener. But things turned sour when photos of the newlyweds with their new favourite confectionery snack were plastered across the magazine, accompanied by a free bar for every reader. A 'traumatised' Anthea hit out at tabloid cries of 'cheap trick' and 'publicity stunt' by insisting it was all a misunderstanding; they'd accidentally posed staring directly at the camera while munching on the chocolatey finger. Only the crumbliest, flakiest celebrity . . .

Jack Ryder and Kym Marsh

Walford's mini-Beckham and Hear'Say's poor man's Posh were destined to tie the knot and boy did they wring every penny out of the occasion. The couple was paid £300,000 by *OK!* for exclusive coverage of their big day and then set about procuring favours from a menswear retailer and a posh hotel to avoid extra expenditure. But Jack's rider back-fired (boom boom!) when the Beeb got peeved at his shameless plugging and fined him to the tune of £20,000 for breach of contract.

Posh and Becks

Putting the 'ewww' into 'nouveau riche' Victoria and David Beckham cadged over £1 million from *OK!* for the exclusive right to photograph their 'fairytale' wedding. Victoria put £10,000 towards a crown and the couple perched, utterly resplendent, atop tasteful gilded thrones. Their special day was accompanied by the dulcet tones of an 18-piece orchestra who played specially rehearsed numbers, including a Spice Girls medley. But the icing on the cake was the arty nude rendering of the golden couple themselves with only fig leaves to cover their modesty. Would you Adam and Eve it?

Johnny Vegas and Kitty Donnelly

Husky-voiced comedian Johnny Vegas had the last laugh when he deliberately avoided having his mug plastered over the leading lifestyle magazines by plumping to sell his wedding photos to *Viz*. In a dashing act of rebellion against the cult of celebrity, Vegas asked for just £5 for the photos but was bargained down to a quid by the wily hacks. The photos featured alongside The Fat Slags and a man with unfeasibly large testicles but Vegas's tasteful alliance came to an end when *Viz* failed to pay up, prompting Vegas to consider legal action to get the pound he'd been promised.

Chris Evans and Billie Piper

Having wasted a fortune on a rose-strewn silver Ferrari for a woman who couldn't drive (she then sold it – good girl!), Chris Evans learnt his lesson and married the humble popstress Billie Piper in a £200 Las Vegas ceremony. The nuptials took place in the Little Church of the West on the Las Vegas strip and were witnessed by none other than Danny 'Daz Doorstep Challenge' Baker – class! Sadly 2004 saw the end of the Evans-Piper union but Evans went on to scale even greater pikey heights by turning his back on his millionaire lifestyle and media mogul career, opting instead to open a second-hand goods stall on Camden market.

Tips from Tinseltown

A great story, attractive lead actors, snappy dialogue – just a few of the essential ingredients for a classic movie. But what filmmakers looking for cinematic longevity and a few golden statuettes on their mantelpiece know is that adding a touch of pikey to the proceedings is what makes a truly great film. What would Oliver Twist have been without the Artful Dodger? The movies are a fantastic resource for anyone looking for pikey inspiration, so crank up the Betamax, watch and learn.

.99p

The Gold Rush

Chaplin's Little Tramp was full of very pikey ideas, but his masterstroke came when he boiled up a shoe for dinner and ate it like he was nibbling on a Ferrero Rocher, making a strong case for the merits of eating pikey food.

Kind Hearts and Coronets

Don't let a little thing like murder get in the way of claiming your rightful place amongst the aristocracy and the fortunes that go with it. If like Louis Manzzini you find yourself disinherited, then ruthless ambition and innovative murder techniques should ensure your humble upbringing is soon a thing of the past.

Risky Business

A classic early Tom Cruise, which traded on his boyish good looks and winning smile to disguise its shady premise – that if you wreck your parents' Porsche, setting up a knocking shop in your own home for the night can be a viable means of raising the money for a new one.

Pretty in Pink

A pikey from the wrong side of the tracks, Andie Walsh was determined to climb the social ladder. One of the early pioneers of Pikeychic™, she transformed her mum's old dress into a glorious prom gown and bagged herself a rich hunk.

Down and Out in Beverly Hills

An example of how to fleece the filthy rich by being a dirty bum. Nick Nolte plays up the idealistic misconception that a vagrant's life is more spiritually fulfilling than living in a mansion (whilst living rent free in a mansion and seducing the host's wife, daughter, maid and even the dog).

Withnail and I

Two 'resting' actors, one free cottage, no food, and lighter fluid instead of booze – a very pikey holiday in the country.

Indecent Proposal

A message to cash-strapped husbands everywhere. Losing everything at the gambling table needn't be the end of the world if you're prepared to let another man boff your missus in exchange for $1 million.

Punch-Drunk Love

Incorporated the true story of a man who collected 1.25 million air miles for just $3,000 worth of puddings, legitimately screwing over a food company's ill-conceived promotion.

Catch Me If You Can

Another real-life tale of a champion scammer who managed to wing it around the world by posing as a variety of professionals and cashing over $2.5 million of fraudulent cheques. Handily, his array of uniforms also proved a hit with the ladies, enabling him to bag more than just the cash.

Money for Old Rope:
How to Be a Modern Artist

'You don't have to be a technical genius to make great art.'
Jeremy Deller, winner of the £25,000 Turner Prize 2004

In these modern times it's not necessary to master the art of the paintbrush, the chisel or the potter's wheel to make it big in the art world. Let's put it this way – you can emulate Michelangelo and spend four years on your back painting the world's most famous mural, or take a leaf out of Tracey Emin's book and mess up your bed, get nominated for the Turner Prize, make the headlines and then have Charles Saatchi take your work of art off your hands for £150,000. Not exactly a taxing decision to be made there. All it takes is the right kind of savvy. But be warned: crap ideas are ten-a-penny; only the great ones will make you a mint. In order to make like a modern artist you have to think like a pikey. Here's how.

.99p

✳ Find art in everyday objects

The first step to becoming a successful modern artist lies in lowering the bar as far as artistic pedigree is concerned. Art is in the eye of the beholder, so if like Marcel Duchamp you think a urinal is worthy of your signature and a place in an exhibition then it is your right to assert this. Oil paints, canvas and giant blocks of marble are expensive raw materials, so it's up to you to fob off bags of rubbish, piles of ashtrays, empty coffee cups and dirty baths as legitimate expression of your most dynamic creative impulses. Generating an air of mystique around your inspiration and working methods should also ensure that people think you are too weird to argue with.

✳ Create an emotional backdrop

Imbuing your work with emotion, childhood recollections or even trauma can turn it into much more than the sum of its parts. Tracey Emin's 'My Bed' is a prime example of this: it is said that the artist recreated it after she'd spent four days in bed contemplating suicide. A year later Emin exhibited a urine-soaked sheet that recalled a mishap on a school trip where she had wet the bed and lay in it paralysed with fear and embarrassment for two days. It's darker than Darth Vader's jockstrap but it certainly worked. Remember the time you ate so many Flying Saucers you puked up fizzy sick? Through your nose? And cried all night through pure humiliation and nasal pain? That's something to work with.

✱ Utilise your bodily functions

A true artist will use anything at their disposal to create their masterpiece. The pikiest amongst them will look to their own waste products to create art that's not only cheap but bound to kick up a bit of a stink. In 1961, whilst living in Milan, Piero Manzoni created ninety cans of Artist's Shit – thirty grams each of freshly tinned excrement straight from his very own back passage. Amazingly, he sold one of them for its own weight in gold. Reports that the other cans ended up in the supermarket reduced section amongst the unlabelled tins are unsubstantiated, although one customer reported his tin of 'beef curry' tasted very strange indeed.

✱ Make a statement about modern life

One of the most pretentious things that you can do as a modern artist is to make a connection between your work and some kind of existential angst. If you can't big up your frugal art with claims of emotional authenticity then it's time to think about its bigger meaning and your place in the scheme of things. Artist Lee Campbell gets second-hand junk and covers it with reduced stickers kindly donated by his local supermarket. He then claims to be making a statement about 'notions of wit and irony in the commercial world we live in' and our 'increasingly depersonalised society'. Some call it bullshitting, we call it deep.

Hire some minions

Andy Warhol had the right idea when he hired a group of assistants willing to do most of the work on his silkscreen prints for him. This allowed him to slack off and oversee the proceedings whilst reclining with a cigar in his mouth, pronouncing to all around that he loves it 'when a plan comes together' (NB: this may not be true). Generating enough kudos to be able to take on a few fawning work-experience students is always a good idea, especially if you can create an exploitative production-line-style factory that churns out your art and you only offer to pay travel expenses from within a one-mile radius.

Create the right reputation

Once you've got a few installations and exhibitions under your belt you can really get to work on your public image. It is essential at this stage to move to the East End of London where you can help perpetuate the romanticised image of the struggling artist on the edge of poverty, even though your last bin bag full of cow dung sold for over fifteen grand. As your confidence grows, so will your brass neck and soon your used colouring-in books will be in the Tate. Finally, like all great creative thinkers, you must master the basics of piss-artistry – all great artists of the past relied on booze for inspiration, so why not see what you can come up with after half a bottle of meths?

He loves modern art and will give you a lot of money for it. Here's his address: write him a letter and he might fix it for you.

The Saatchi Gallery
County Hall
Southbank
London
SE1 7PB

MR CHARLES SAATCHI
THE SAATCHI GALLERY
COUNTY HALL
SOUTHBANK
LONDON
SE1 7PB

DEAR CHARLES

The Pikey in Vogue

CHEAP!

You could be forgiven for thinking that the fashionistas and the pikeys are more bitterly opposed than the Scorpions and the T-Birds, when in truth the world of fashion has always been a dedicated follower of pikey. Like Audrey Hepburn or Jackie O, the pikey has been a muse for designers and trendsetters throughout the ages, who return time and again to the thrown-together just-got-out-of-bed look for inspiration.

The pikey boho look of juxtaposed styles and textures has recently found an ardent champion in Sarah Jessica Parker, who influenced the resurrection of many a discarded tutu and generated a waiting list for name necklaces at Elizabeth Duke. The pikey is not a slave to style and will decide what to wear every day with a quick spin of their favourite childhood toy: the Fashion Wheel. Indeed, Sienna Miller and Kate Moss have both recently been spotted with this indispensable style tool tucked under their arm. But the Primrose Hill set are not the only celebrities to embrace Pikeychic™ . . .

Jenny and Jimmy

Now then, now then, boys and girls. Brightly coloured shell suits, coupled with bling and golden locks. Sound familiar? Jennifer Lopez looked to our very own Sir Jimmy Savile for fashion inspiration and took it back to The Block. Rumours have it that Jen's now also partial to the odd cigar and has penned a new single entitled 'Jingle Jangle – How's About That Then?'

David and Mahatma

When Posh suggested getting an Indian in, Beckham returned from Blockbusters armed with the highly acclaimed biopic, *Gandhi*. Impressed with Gandhi's selfless, non-materialistic life, Beckham thought he'd emulate him and was straight down Harvey Nicks to buy a sarong, although he quickly discarded the flipflops after missing a crucial penalty against France in Euro 2004.

Britney and Waynetta

Once the squeaky-clean princess of pop, now a scruffy, chain-smoking, greasy-haired rebel who looks in need of a good bath. Could it be that Britney is the new Waynetta? Ms Spears is not a stranger to a slobby tracksuit or the odd fag and has been spotted quaffing miniatures on the street. And now that she's sprogged up, it would seem like life really does imitate art.

⭐ Sean and Del

Whilst channel-hopping in his palatial crib, P. Diddy couldn't believe his eyes when he stumbled upon a re-run of *Only Fools and Horses* on UKTV Gold. 'Peckham Fabulous!' he exclaimed. Why hadn't he thought of the sheepskin and bling combination before? P. Diddy was last seen doing wheel spins in a Reliant Robin.

⭐ Badly and Compo

Which is which?

After consulting the Fashion Wheel, we have predicted that the following trends will grace the catwalk in 2006.

For men: the Columbo mac, cor blimey trousers and Chas 'n' Dave-style neckerchiefs and braces.

For the ladies: Fergie bows, Jimmy Krankie-style grey school shorts, and black patent leather shoes with adaptable slingback straps.

You saw it here first.

£40.00

The Future of Pikey

Survival of the Pikiest:
Evolution and the Überpikey

A controversial new theory has suggested that, should the nuclear apocalypse ever come to fruition, only two species will survive to battle for supremacy on Planet Earth: the cockroach and the Überpikey. Some scientists have argued that Cher will be there too, but further research is needed to determine whether she could then survive an attack of the roaches. In any case, it is commonly agreed amongst the world's foremost thinkers that the evolution of the pikey into something resembling a gigantic goggle-eyed shelled insect is inevitable.

.99p

Pikeys are unlike any other breed of human being, such as the Scouser or the *Cosmopolitan* reader, and have the capacity to evolve at a much faster rate. Their genetic state having been permanently altered by over-consumption of food additives and sheer devotion to pikeyness, they will undergo this drastic physical transformation in order to optimise their pikey potential and make everyday life that little bit more convenient.

The first notable change will be the metamorphosis of the skin into a hardened layer, until finally the Überpikey has developed a shiny shell. This will liberate them from the need to wear clothes or even waste money on housing, since come hell or high water the Überpikey will be protected and able to withstand extreme degrees of heat or cold. This shell will also make for great armour against fellow jostlers in the Christmas sales or at the bric-a-brac stall. Unlike the cockroach, however, the Überpikey will have handy little pockets in their shell, convenient for secreting away their pikey finds from the prying eyes (or antennae) of others.

The arms and legs will be transformed as they grow much longer, thinner and develop spiky hairs. This added length will enable the Überpikey, when poised on its rear legs, to reach over the heads of others to grab bargains at the supermarket as well as outrun policemen should their thieving ways land them outside of the law. Eventually, the Überpikey will develop an extra set of limbs which can double as legs or arms and will be dead useful down the Cash 'n' Carry. Pointy knees and elbows will act as jabs to negotiate crowds, and claws instead of fingers will enable the Überpikey to climb up walls, open canned corned beef by hand and hitch free intercontinental lifts by attaching themselves to the outsides of aeroplanes.

The most noticeable change in the pikey's facial features will come with the enlargement of the eyes, which will become as big as Fray Bentos pie tins and capable of looking in two directions at the same time. The Überpikey will develop impeccable long-distance vision in order to spot a bargain from a mile off, and with highly developed olfactory nerves will be able to smell them too. Conversely, the mouth will shrink so that the Überpikey is unable to overeat and spend excessive amounts on food on a regular basis. Like the cockroach, the Überpikey will be able to survive for a month without eating but will eat like a king should free food be on offer. A detachable jaw will ensure that, should a free buffet situation arise, the Überpikey can stuff as much food into its mouth as possible without cutting it up, handy for eating entire roast chickens in one go.

The Überpikey will be able to survive in the most unhygienic of conditions which, given their propensity to hoard things and not bother cleaning, will be a real bonus. They will spend up to 80 per cent of their time resting and the remainder in the gleeful pursuit of bargains and free stuff. Like the cockroach, the Überpikey will be able to live for up to a week without its head. Its downfall will only come about because without its eyes the Überpikey will be unable to read *Loot* or the Argos catalogue and will die of a broken heart.

Pikey Patents

Being an inventor like Caractacus Potts is a great way of avoiding a proper job and may even lead to striking the jackpot, should your invention be picked up by a major corporation. Now that the world is more open to the possibilities of pikey, we're hoping some of these little gems from the patent vaults will go into production.

.99p

Pikey Patent #1:
The Tricycle Lawnmower
US Patent 4,455,816

It's all very well feeding your child on cheap food chock full of sugar and additives, but what to do when they're climbing the walls as a result? The answer to every lazy parent's prayers, this ingenious tricycle lawnmower harnesses the power of a child wired on E-numbers to fulfil a vital gardening function, thus unburdening everyone involved. Never mind the hazardous aspect of placing your little one on a bike with blades, once the neighbours clock this little beauty you'll be able to hire it out, complete with child, and make a fortune on the side. A little hard work never did anyone any harm, and the sooner the pikelet learns that, the better.

FIG. 1

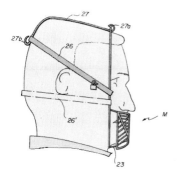

Pikey Patent #2:
Anti-Eating Mouth Cage
US Patent 4,344,424

Overeating not only poses various risks for one's health but can be equally detrimental to the wallet. A pork pie here, a slice of bread and dripping there, the odd left-over curry – not only does this culinary overindulgence cost a fortune but you'll inevitably have to fork out on a bigger pair of trousers too. What better way to make expensive snacking habits a thing of the past than by barricading your mouth with this anti-eating cage? Not only will your food bills be cut in half but you can also put the frighteners on the milkman by donning a boiler suit and doing a very convincing Hannibal Lecter impression.

Pikey Patent #3:
The Horse-Powered Minibus
UK Patent Application No. GB2060081

Quite why the inventors of this outlandish mode of transport thought it would be preferable to the plain yet reliable old horse and cart is beyond our

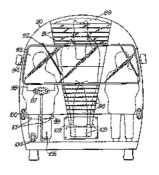

comprehension. Nevertheless it's hard not to admire the thought that's gone into this horse-powered minibus and how cool it would be to own one. Said horse stands in a compartment and powers the wheels of the bus by trotting on a conveyor belt, while the driver steers the bus. If the nag gets too hot from all this hard work, there's even a control on the dashboard to mop his sweaty brow. How thoughtful.

Pikey Patent #4:
The Portable Seat
UK Patent Application No. GB2267208

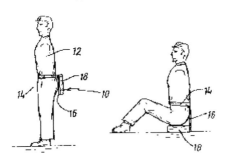

Not necessarily inspired by pikey-ness itself but more an incredibly useful tool for those of a pikey disposition, the strap-on portable seat is a miracle of transportable furniture. You see, it costs a great deal of money to furnish a house with enough seating – a sofa for the lounge, dining-room chairs, stools for the kitchen – but by having a cushion attached to one's derriere the problem is solved. When guests arrive at your house simply furnish them with a seat and they are able to recline wherever they wish around the house in complete comfort without requiring expensive, extensive seating. Pure genius, we're sure you'll agree.

Pikey Patent #5:
The Bird-Powered Blimp
US Patent 363,037

Flying a blimp from A to B can be a real bummer when a gust of wind sends you careering off course. But why spend money on expensive engines that require fuel and upkeep? Surely there must be another way? The obvious solution would be to engage the services of a couple of large birds (some eagles, condors or vultures perhaps) to help power the blimp and aid in steering it to your intended destination. The birds are strapped to the top of the balloon and, indulging their wish to fly away, power the blimp. It's then up to the driver to steer them in the right direction, using the handle attached to their perches. Home, James! And don't spare the . . . birds.

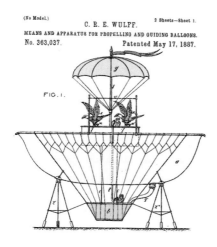

(No Model.)   2 Sheets—Sheet 1.

C. R. E. WULFF.

MEANS AND APPARATUS FOR PROPELLING AND GUIDING BALLOONS.

No. 363,037.   Patented May 17, 1887.

FIG. 1.

Pikey Patent #6:
The Dad Saddle
US Patent 6,365,765

It's a win-win situation for the cash-strapped Dad and lazy child when Dad dons the Dad Saddle. The most pikey amongst dads would put the Saddle on their child and hitch a lift down to the pub, expecting said child to wait outside for three hours with a cola and a bag of peanuts before taking pissed Dad back home again.

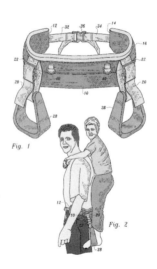

Fig. 1

Fig. 2

CHEAP!

Questionnaire

Now that you're fully acquainted with the way of the pikey it's time for a moment of introspection, during which you're likely to ask yourself some important questions, like why did I spend £9.99 on this book? But relax, dear reader, it's time to clear your mind and embark on a voyage of self-discovery with our pikey questionnaire. Using a scientifically proven formula, our system will accurately measure how pikey you are by pinpointing where your strengths and weaknesses lie. Just study the questions and carefully pick the most appropriate answer, then let the pike-o-meter do the hard work for you.

.99p

In your wallet you have:

a) A platinum credit card and a wodge of fifty-pound notes.
b) A bank card, a bit of cash, a library card and a photo of your cat.
c) No money, no bank card, but loyalty cards with enough points to survive cash-free for two years. And someone else's Giro.

You have furnished your home with:

a) Family heirlooms, the odd piece from Sotheby's and knickknacks from your travels abroad.
b) A few bits you've splashed out on and your Nan's old table, but mostly durable, reasonably priced Swedish stuff.
c) Furniture from other people's front gardens, traffic cones, and chairs stolen from service stations.

What do you eat for breakfast?

a) Potted shrimp on toast.
b) Cereal or fruit.
c) The kebab in the fridge that you stole from a tramp and have been picking at all week.

Your perfect job involves:

a) Earning pots of money, regardless of its toll on your family/friends/heart.
b) Having enough time and money to enjoy life to the full.
c) Acquiring as many freebies and perks as possible whilst

writing most of your outgoings off as expenses on your tax return and moonlighting as a smuggler.

To send a letter you:

a) Put a stamp on it and get the PA to put it in a post box, of course.
b) Take it to work and put it in the post tray.
c) Steam open old mail, re-seal your letter inside and write instructions for it to be re-directed to the desired address.

Charity fund-raising is:

a) A great way to raise a few pounds for those less fortunate than yourself.
b) A chore, but all your friends do it.
c) A prime opportunity to scam some money for the greatest charity of all – yourself.

You stay in touch with old relatives because:

a) You love them.
b) They're slightly batty and smell a bit, but they've always been kind to you.
c) They won't hold out much longer and then, bingo! – it's inheritance time.

What do you look for in a partner?

a) Class, style, looks and a title.
b) Looks, a sense of humour and a low expectation threshold.

c) A house that you can live in, clothes that fit you and good life insurance.

How do you keep up with the latest fashion?

a) By cruising Bond Street.
b) By looking for high-street copies.
c) By bartering at your local charity shop.

You've been coerced into a trip to a reputable pizza restaurant. Which pizza do you choose?

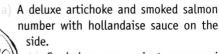

a) A deluxe artichoke and smoked salmon number with hollandaise sauce on the side.
b) Go halves on a giant pepperoni gut-buster with your friend.
c) Whichever, after close inspection with a tape measure and pair of scales, works out to be the most cost efficient.

What do the colours red, white and blue bring to mind?

a) Kieslowski's transcendent *Three Colours* trilogy.
b) Geri Halliwell's Union Jack dress.
c) The divine simplicity of the Tesco Value range.

Going to a party, do you:

a) Take a decent bottle of wine to impress your friends and potential lovers, probably something from the cellar or some Bolly.

b) Take screw-top wine that you won on the tombola.

c) Take screw-top wine that would melt the linoleum and stick an expensive price label on it. Then drink all the vodka.

You will spend money on:

a) Living the high life and making sure everybody is jealous.

b) Living comfortably.

c) Spend? What? Ha!

The Results:

Mostly As

What ho! We suspect you have far too much money and are frittering it away at a rate of knots. You live in one of the many mansions that you inherited, drive a flash car, and have more diamonds than the ground floor of Tiffany's. You get an itchy rash just thinking about Argos and think plus-fours are very fashionable. But are you fulfilled? Happiness isn't something you can ring the butler for, you know. There's fun to be had in being pikey and it's there for the taking. Think of the money you'll save. Bonkers!

Mostly Bs

You're the Ken Barlow of the pikey world: you wear beige jumpers with leather elbow patches, live in a Barratt home and listen to Phil Collins. You subscribe to the *Reader's Digest* and regularly order from the Innovations catalogue. In your mind, living on the edge is incurring a library fine on Tony Parsons' latest *chef d'oeuvre*, but have you ever thought you

need to get out more? Where's your sense of adventure? Live life on the wild side, stay on the bus for an extra stop you haven't paid for and eat all the biscuits at the vicar's tea party.

Mostly Cs

Hmmm . . . have we met before? Your pikeyness is on a par with the Artful Dodger, so greatly honed are your wily ways. You're on first-name terms with your local bus driver and head the list of the most wanted at the Benefits Office. Cries of 'skip rat' and 'bin scab' follow you wherever you go but that still doesn't deter you from stealing from your neighbour's washing line. You are to Lidl what Jamie Oliver is to Sainsbury's and you've eaten so much Spam it's altered your genetic make-up. You're so pikey you knew exactly what this book was about before we even wrote it.

Pikey Manifesto

Let us not wallow in the valley of despair. We say to you, our pikey friends, even though we face the difficulties of today and tomorrow, we still have a dream. It's a dream deeply rooted in our love of a bargain.

.99p

We have a dream that one day this nation will rise up and free itself from the shackles of needless consumerism and live out the true meaning of pikeyness. So we have come to cash this cheque – a cheque with a wobbly signature on it – that will give us upon demand the riches we so rightly deserve for a lifetime's toil at the coalface of capitalism. We have a dream today.

We have a dream that one day even High Street Kensington, a street melting under the heat of so many credit-card transactions, will be transformed into an oasis of pawnbrokers and charity shops. We have a dream that one day in the aisles of Asda the sons of eBay dealers and the sons of freeloading aristos will buy the same low-priced sausages.

We have a dream that one day our children will live in a nation where they will not be judged by the clothes they wear but by their vast array of cunning money-making scams. And our children's children will still be wearing hand-me-downs that we were fifth in line for ourselves.

This is our hope. With this hope we will be able to transform the disillusionment of our nation into a beautiful symphony of pikey contentment. With this new hope we will be able to skive work together, get two cups of tea out of one teabag together, get locked up for tax evasion together, start sham charities together, knowing that it's much better than spending our hard-earned cash and time without a second thought.

This is the day when life has new meaning, and if Great Britain is to be a really great nation then this must become true. So let the phrase 'Pikey and Proud!' ring from every cut-price supermarket and every bingo hall, from every car boot sale and every reclamation centre. From the hearts of the dispossessed and disenfranchised, let pikey ring.

When this happens, when we allow ourselves to revel in our true pikey status, when we gather in sub-zero temperatures for first dibs in the January sales, when we holiday last-minute to God-knows-where, when we dig out our rollerskates to avoid the congestion charge, we will be bringing closer that day when all of pikeykind will be able to join hands and sing in the words of the pikey spiritual, 'Pikey at last! Pikey at last! Thank God Almighty, we are pikey at last!'

Glossary

Bargain   The essence of the pikey shopping experience. Must be attained at all costs and cannot be resisted.

Bargain-basement   The Promised Land, where pikeys are free to be who they want to be, and do what they want to do.

Bartering   A form of conversational manipulation in which a pikey will aggressively appeal for the price of a product that they desire to be lowered.

Bin-Diver   Urban beachcomber whose pickings come from the refuse of others, especially celebrities, whose trash can be sold to the tabloids for a sum.

Bludge   To scrounge from someone else something you have no intention of returning.

BYOB   Bring your own booze – a sign of a stingy host.

Cheap-Jack   A dealer in cheap and often ripped-off merchandise. Also an adjective: very, very cheap.

Cheapskate   One whose sole philosophy is to do things on the cheap. Will never spend more than necessary, whatever the consequences. May also wear skates.

Cheeseparer   Relating to the separation of cheese from its rind, indicating that trying to get money out of one of these people is like getting blood out of a stone.

Churl	A medieval peasant. In modern usage, a being of ill-breeding whose stinginess knows no bounds and who is absolutely miserable.
Economy	The state in which a pikey chooses to exist, intentionally saving money. Also a word emblazoned on the packaging of anything the pikey might buy.
Floater	A worker who moves from place to place, and job to job, often to avoid tax. May try to pass themselves off as a 'freelancer' – read 'freeloader'.
Freebie	The Holy Grail of pikey living.
Gold-Digger	One whose sole purpose in dating and mating is to improve their financial outlook. Feigns love to get cash. Usually very clever.
Hoarder	One who amasses objects others would deem useless on the off chance they might one day be useful or profitable.
Hunks	A type of miser who is incredibly surly and bad-tempered. Not to be confused with a hunk, who looks so good nobody cares if he's surly or not.
Idler	One with no apparent means of employment, who spends his or her days exerting as little effort as possible, to the envy of all of their friends.
Lady of leisure	A female of the species who occupies herself with leisure pursuits such as shopping, pampering and socialising when everyone else is at work.
Loafing	The conservation of energy and resources achieved by not exerting oneself in any way, thus not going out to work.
Miser	From the Latin *miser* meaning miserable. Someone who hates spending money.
Niggard	One who covets anything and everything but whose

meanness leads to a deep and bitter form of stinginess.

Parsimony	A penchant for economising, or being stingy.
Penury	An extreme form of stinting and often niggardly frugality.
Piker	Australian slang for a person who avoids work, also one who will only speculate small amounts of money whilst gambling.
Prudence	Mind over matter: namely the ability to control one's spending habits and exercise skill and shrewdness in managing financial affairs.
Ragbag	Originally a bag for scraps of, you guessed it . . . rags. Now applied to those who employ an eclectic attitude towards dressing.
Road Agent	A highwayman who operated on stage routes of troubled locales. Is now employed in the insurance industry.
Rogue	Often 'loveable rogue'. One incapable of good behaviour who somehow manages to make mischief, endearing to those who don't know any better.
Scab	The art of procuring a cigarette when you have none of your own. Usually followed by the question, 'Got a light?'
Scally	Pikey miscreant originating from the area of Liverpool, usually male and very arrogant. Wearer of Nike leisurewear and Rockport boots.
Scav	Abbreviation of the word scavenge, often prefixed by skip or bin.
Scrimping	The art of economising, saving money when providing something, for instance in making clothes that tiny bit too small or serving very small portions at a dinner party.
Scrooge	From Dickens's *A Christmas Carol*. One whose miserliness extends to the mistreatment of others.

Shrewd	A wily wheeler-dealer given to making up scams and artful plans which nearly always work. A great threat to those of little intelligence.
Shylock	From Shakespeare's *The Merchant of Venice*. Moneylender who makes a mint by extorting massive interest rates out of borrowers. See: Bank.
Skinflint	A close relative of the pikey who will save, extort, or gain money by any means possible.
Skip Rats	Those who take advantage of another's hired skip either to fill it with their own rubbish during the night or rifle through what's there and steal it.
Spam-Eater	A fan of the cheap foodstuff Spam: a tinned plethora of animal parts with various culinary uses but whose origins are dubious.
Sponging	The art of avoiding the workplace, achieved by imposing on the hospitality or generosity of another, especially the state.
Tatter-demalion	One dressed in ragged clothing.
Tight-Arse	One whose methods of saving resources are manifested in a physical affliction: the tightening of the sphincter.
Tight-Fisted	A state similar to yet less painful than that experienced by the tight-arse, this time afflicting the fist, often grasped around money with which the owner refuses to part.
Twofor	Slang for 'two for the price of one' offers.

Acknowledgements

Barbara and Tony Bushell, Blue Witch, Cameron, Deptford, Henry Jeffreys, Jocasta Brownlee, Juliet Brightmore, Kevin Conroy-Scott, Nolan's, Mac and Linda, Ted VanCleave at www.totallyabsurd.com, Tim Jackson and all the residents of 19 Lansdowne Gardens past and present.

Picture Acknowledgements
Photographs © Carrie-Anne Brackstone and Laura Bushell

Additional Sources
©Corbis: pages 2/Poodles Rock, 12/Archivo Iconographica SA, 20/Grant Smith, 28/Strauss Curtis, 65/Bennett Dean, 96/Jerry Schaltzberg, 106/Henry Diltz, 138/NASA, 142/Jim Cornfield, 150/Kieran Doherty/Reuters
©Corbis/Bettman: pages 16, 18, 20, 24, 26, 62, 122
© Corbis/Hulton-Deutch Collection: pages 8, 130
©Getty Images/Hulton Archive: pages 48, 74, 76, 79
©Rex Features: pages 88/Tony Kryiacou, 108, 118/Everett Collection, 132/MB Pictures, 133 left, 133 right/Mark Campbell